SALMON IS EVERYTHING

Community-Based Theatre in the Klamath Watershed

SECOND EDITION

FIRST PEOPLES
New Directions in Indigenous Studies

Other volumes in the
First Peoples: New Directions in Indigenous Studies Series

Accomplishing NAGPRA: Perspectives on the Intent, Impact, and Future of the Native American Graves Protection and Repatriation Act
Edited by Sangita Chari and Jaime M. N. Lavallee

Ancestral Places: Understanding Kanaka Geographies
Katrina-Ann R. Kapāʻanaokalāokeola Nākoa Oliveira

Asserting Native Resilience: Pacific Rim Indigenous Nations Face the Climate Crisis
Edited by Zoltán Grossman and Alan Parker

At the Hearth of the Crossed Races: A French-Indian Community in Nineteenth-Century Oregon, 1812–1859
Melinda Marie Jetté

A Deeper Sense of Place: Stories and Journeys of Collaboration in Indigenous Research
Edited by Jay T. Johnson and Soren C. Larsen

The Indian School on Magnolia Avenue: Voices and Images from Sherman Institute
Edited by Clifford E. Trafzer, Matthew Sakiestewa Gilbert, and Lorene Sisquoc

Kanaka Hawaiʻi Cartography: Hula, Navigation, and Oratory
Renee Pualani Louis with Moana Kahele

Native Space: Geographic Strategies to Unsettle Settler Colonialism
Natchee Blu Barnd

Songs of Power and Prayer in the Columbia Plateau: The Jesuit, the Medicine Man, and the Indian Hymn Singer
Chad S. Hamill

To Win the Indian Heart: Music at Chemawa Indian School
Melissa D. Parkhurst

SALMON IS EVERYTHING

Community-Based Theatre in the Klamath Watershed

SECOND EDITION

THERESA MAY

with

Suzanne Burcell

Kathleen McCovey

Marta Lu Clifford

Jean O'Hara

Kirby Brown

FOREWORD BY GORDON BETTLES

Oregon State University Press Corvallis

FIRST PEOPLES

New Directions in Indigenous Studies

The Library of Congress has cataloged the first edition as follows:

May, Theresa J.
Salmon is everything: community-based theatre from the klamath watershed / Theresa May with Suzanne Burcell, Kathleen McCovey, and Jean O'Hara; foreword by Gordon Bettles.
p. cm.
Includes bibliographical references and index.
ISBN 978-0-87071-746-8 (alk. paper)—ISBN 978-0-87071-747-5 (e-book)
1. Klamath Indians—Fishing 2. Klamath Indians—Social life and customs. 3. Salmon—Spawning—Klamath River Watershed (Or. and Calif.) 4. Salmon fisheries—Klamath River Watershed (Or. and Calif.) 5. Indian theater—Klamath River Watershed (Or. and Calif.) 6. American drama—Klamath River Watershed (Or. and Calif.)—Indian authors. 7. Klamath River Watershed (Or. and Calif.)—Social life and customs.
E99.K7M39 2014
979.5'2—dc23
2013041306

♾ This paper meets the requirements of ANSI/NISO Z39.48-1992 (Permanence of Paper).

ISBN 978-0-87071-947-9

First edition published 2014 by Oregon State University Press
Second edition 2018
Printed in the United States of America

Oregon State University Press
121 The Valley Library
Corvallis OR 97331-4501
541-737-3166 • fax 541-737-3170
www.osupress.oregonstate.edu

Cover Photo: Mary Campbell and Jason Tower in the 2006 production of *Salmon Is Everything* at Humboldt State University. Photo: Kellie Brown.

pa'aama kumá'ii
mehl kue ney-puy
mah łoq' aiundidé
č'iya.l'sy.i
for the sake of the Salmon

ACKNOWLEDGMENTS

My heart is filled with gratitude to the many people whose support, inspiration and contributions are part of this book and the play it contains. Big thanks to thank all who participated in the development of *Salmon Is Everything*—members of the Karuk, Yurok, Hoopa Valley, and Klamath Tribes, the Klamath Watershed community, and the students, faculty, and staff of Humboldt State and the University of Oregon, who are acknowledged by name in the credits to the play that is part of this volume. I am deeply grateful to my fellow collaborators, Jean O'Hara, Suzanne Burcell and Kathleen McCovey, whose essays appear in this volume, who read portions of the manuscript and offered wise suggestions as well as encouragement; and to this edition's new contributors, Kirby Brown and Marta Lu Clifford, for their spirit of generosity, faith, and numerous insights. Neither this volume nor the play it contains would have been possible without the support and good people at Humboldt State University including Rollin Richmond, Denice Helwig, Marlon and Dale Ann Sherman, Lyn Risling, the Environment and Community Program; and the staff of the Indian Tribal and Educational Personnel Program, including Phil Zastrow, Judy Risling, and Marlette Grant-Jackson. Several friends and colleagues at Humboldt State served as a sounding board for ideas and challenges or read portions of the manuscript, including Margaret Kelso, Linda Sievers, Sharon Butcher, Christina Accomondo, Eric Rofes, Mary Virnoche, Josh Meisel, John Meyer, and Nicole Barchilon Frank. Heartfelt gratitude also belongs to colleagues at the University of Oregon who encouraged this project and provided insightful comments and advice, in particular Gordon Bettles, Tom and Alison Ball, Kirby Brown, Brian Klopotek, Jennifer O'Neal, Kari Norgaard, Jules Bacon, Melina Pastos, Linda Forrest, Debra Merskin, Adell Amos, Michael Najjar, Olga Sanchez Saltveit, Zeina Salame, and the Native Strategies Group—it's an honor indeed to be your colleague. I'm grateful for the support of colleagues and administrators at the University of Oregon, including Karen Ford, Henry

Wonham, Doug Blandy, Barbara Altmann, and Julia Heydon; and to the Oregon Humanities Center, College of Arts and Sciences, UO's Many Nations Longhouse, Center for the Study of Women and Society, and Department of Theatre Arts—all of which provided both moral and financial support for this book. Julian Lang, Ducayne Arwood, Silischaitawn Jackson, and James Gensaw assisted with the dedication translation; Craig Tucker, Natural Resources Policy, Karuk Tribe; Konrad Fisher, Klamath Riverkeeper; and Terrence Malcolm offered key advice; and Mike Neuman at the Klamath office of the US Bureau of Reclamation provided maps and figures. Barry McCovey Jr. and Becky Hatfield Hyde are cited in the text of the play where their words animate the characters of Tim, Alice, and Will; I am grateful for their generosity and willingness to review pertinent portions of this manuscript. Much gratitude to Mary Elizabeth Braun at Oregon State University Press for approaching me about the possibility of a book such as this, and for her patient and helpful suggestions throughout its development, and to the entire OSU Press editorial staff. Lastly, a shout out of gratitude to José Cruz González for his open-hearted dramaturgy early in the process, and to Julie Pearson-Little Thunder, who read early drafts and gave candid good counsel. Neither the first edition nor this one would have been possible with the faith of my husband, Larry Fried, who helps me remember that we are part of a precious ecological community.

There is no convenient place in this list to thank the many Grandmothers who made meals, sat through rehearsals, gave rides, loaned regalia and cultural objects, and gave freely of their wisdom and knowledge: we were honored by your presence; your acts of generosity made this work possible. Thank you.

CONTENTS

FOREWORD

When Cultures Collide

Gordon Bettles

The historic fish kill on the Lower Klamath River in autumn 2002 was an example of what can happen when cultures collide in the Pacific Northwest. Members of the Karuk, Yurok, Hoopa Valley, and Klamath Indian Tribes protested at the time, claiming that the die-off of chinook and coho salmon was a threat to cultural traditions, food sources, and spiritual life. We demonstrated scientifically that high water temperatures, low water levels, and toxic algae levels caused by the overuse of water by agriculture were the material causes of the fish kill. Warnings had been given in spring 2001 by Native scientists and in reports made to the Environmental Protection Agency (EPA) by the National Marine Fisheries Service and other agencies. But when the EPA made its ruling in favor of salmon, farmers and ranchers in the Klamath County agricultural areas staged their own protests, and ultimately, the federal government reversed its position, giving farmers in eastern Oregon the water they claimed they needed to maintain their own economic survival.

The tragedy of the 2002 fish kill was caused by a collision of cultures that began when the first ships landed on the east coast of North America in 1492. At the heart of that collision are two creation stories that give rise to two distinct ways of relating to the natural world. I am a member of the Klamath Tribes of south-central Oregon. As with most tribes, our Klamath legends begin with a creation story. The Klamath tell how Gmok'amc (pronounced *ga mo k'amch*), or Old Man of the Ancient Ones, caused the land to rise above the waters of the ocean. He caused Gopher to open his mouth. All manner of flora and fauna jumped out of Gopher's mouth and began to seek out the places in the world where they could live. Trees found the mountains and the hills, while grasses found they could live almost anywhere. Some sought to live along the rivers and lakes, while some even decided they could live in the waters. The animals made choices on how they could live and thrive in this world. Elk, deer and the other animals chose what they could eat and where they wanted to live. Birds flew out and found their homes to be in trees, in caves, or in the ground, while some preferred to live at the edges of the great waters of the world. Fish jumped out of Gopher's mouth and sought the waters of the world. Among them was *č'iyals* (pronounced *cheey-als*), or Salmon, who chose to live in the Big Water as well as in the rivers and lakes. Soon after, Gmok'amc created the Klamath people from the *čak*, or Service Berry bush.

The Klamath people give prayers of thanks to Gmok'amc and to the other life forms before planting, gathering, hunting, fishing, and utilizing these abundant resources. Tribal elders caution all to not overharvest these resources and to always leave some here and there so the plants can come back the next year. The Klamath Seasonal Round begins in August, when the *wocas*, or water lily seed pods, are gathered for processing, followed by big game hunting and house-building time. The winter season is filled with some hunting and fishing, but mostly legend-telling time, tool building, and weaving. The next great season comes with the return of the *c'wam*, or sucker fish. The c'wam ceremony is held yearly to give thanks to these fish for returning to the Klamath River. A similar ceremony celebrated the return of Salmon to the waterways of south-central Oregon and northern California, but in the twentieth century dams placed in the Klamath River have barred the Salmon from the Klamath Basin, and our Salmon ceremony has become a distant memory. The berry-picking season is followed by the root-gathering time, after which the Klamath people return to the lakes and marshes to begin gathering wocas.

The survival of the Klamath people has depended on these food resources for thousands of years. All these foods are considered a gift from the Creator and to not give thanks for them is considered an insult. Likewise, hunters are taught to give thanks to the spirit of the deer that are killed for providing sustenance to the tribe. Legends still tell about some of the animal people eating c'wam without prayers and then lying to Gmok'amc about it. Gmok'amc turns them to stone, and these rock features can be seen in the landscape today. Foods to be eaten are also placed outside to feed the ancestors. Elders teach that the gift of food should never be put in an unclean place. All are requested to drink *ambo* (water) before eating to clean their palate. These everyday practices have been passed down from generation to generation.

In contrast, the newcomers' creation story, as told in their Holy Bible, gave people dominion over all others who dwell in the world and instructed them to tame the creatures into service. Dogs, cats, goats, cattle, sheep, horses, and other animals were domesticated according to these directives. When the newcomers arrived in the so-called New World, this story informed the way they saw the land and its communities. The natural resources—animals, vegetation, waters, minerals—seemed endless in this new land. It seemed to beg to be conquered, to be tamed, the newcomers thought. The land needed to be tilled, the meadows fenced, the waterways controlled, the mountains dug and mined. Transposed onto the New World, the newcomers' creation story unleashed a harmful dynamic between people and the land, and one that was very different from the story that had sustained the tribes for thousands of years. Believing the land was a resource, a commodity to be harnessed for the good of mankind, the newcomers fell into a pattern of exploitation without self-regulation.

The differences in cultural perspectives between the Klamath people and the newcomers have played out through the twentieth century to the present collision over the fate of the Salmon and the River itself.[1] The newcomers view natural resources as materials to exploit, while the Klamath people (and other tribal peoples in our watershed) understand that Creator provided for people to use these resources in a respectful and sustainable manner, with the knowledge that people and what the newcomers call "nature" are one. The play *Salmon Is Everything* shows these different perspectives and the cost of treating the natural world as a commodity.

The loss of thirty-four thousand lives in such a short time in September 2002 was nearly inconceivable to us. We knew something was terribly wrong. The Klamath, Modoc, Yahooskin, Karuk, Hupa, and Yurok people have sustained ourselves and our environment for thousands of years.[2] The newcomers brought different values and definitions of success to our homeland, but at what cost? The death of thousands of chinook was a signal not only that the manipulated Klamath River could not sustain the Salmon (who were simply doing what they were created to do), but also that the newcomers' perspective and way of treating the world is unsustainable. *Salmon Is Everything* shows the results of two distinct ways of viewing the world and expresses some of what we felt, showing how Indian communities of the Klamath watershed were bound together against a wall of collective grief. When that event occurred, the Klamath Tribes and our neighboring tribes to the south felt a terrible pain and sadness not only for our immediate loss, but for what it seemed to mean for the future of our culture, the Salmon, and the River.

Death has particular cultural meanings for the Klamath people, and the deaths of so many Salmon must be understood in light of two Klamath words. *Gleega*, "death," means literally to change into or become something else. This is a natural process, a change that transforms life into life. In contrast, *č'ooq'atk* means "dead ones," or corpses, and refers to unnatural loss, such as a murder, or multiple deaths that are outside the natural order. The distinction lies in what *caused* the death. Was it caused by the Creator and part of a natural phenomenon, or was it caused by human action or error? In the case of the fish kill, we asked, what could take *hoqis*, or life, away from this many Salmon at once? We could see that this was an unnatural event, caused by human values and practices. The tribes could understand if such a catastrophe had been caused by a natural process, such as a volcanic event. We believe that in such a case the Salmon would adapt to the change in the environment, or move to a new one. But the assault on the River and its environs was tantamount to a mugging—*č'ooq'atk*. It should never have happened.

The creation story of the newcomers allows them to believe that while the loss of so many Salmon was unfortunate, it was somehow unavoidable. Humans and their needs should come first over the fish. The release of upstream water had to be withheld no matter the cost because farmers and ranchers and their livelihoods were in danger due to drought. After all, raising cattle and potatoes made more economic sense to them than the tribes' need for fishing. Besides, the tribes could go to the local supermarket and purchase farm-raised salmon. But for the tribes, the Salmon represents more than a food source; it represents the continuation of the world as the Creator intended. The fish runs were predictable; food was promised and given. The tribes know that this was what the Creator intended for them. They also know that the Salmon in turn knows his way home and has the intention of supplying himself to the people for their sustenance. This is why the spirit of the Salmon is thanked in prayer and ceremonies. But now the situation for the Klamath River Salmon is dire: the fish kill of 2002 was a warning about the real possibility of extinction.

Our treaties with the US government guarantee the tribes their right to fish, hunt, and gather in our homelands. Yet mismanagement has eroded and threatened those rights. The dams built in the twentieth century have blocked the Salmon for such a long time that many newcomers in the Upper Klamath Basin do not believe that the Salmon ever came this far inland, up into the Klamath Watershed. When the fossilized remains of a six-foot king salmon were found in an archaeological dig in Chiloquin, Oregon, there was no doubt that the Salmon had been traveling those 400-plus miles from the Pacific Ocean to continue living and doing what they were created to do since time immemorial. Now, land managers, politicians, lawyers, farmers, ranchers, and economists can see what the tribes have known all along: the Salmon belong in the Klamath watershed, from its beginning at the Pacific Ocean to its headwaters in eastern Oregon. *Salmon Is Everything* is an example of what can be done to help bridge the cultures that collided in the Klamath watershed. But the play is only part of a larger drama that is still unfolding, one that will not be complete until the dams on the Klamath River are decommissioned and taken down, and the Salmon that once flourished throughout the watershed are allowed to return.

Gordon Bettles
Eugene, Oregon
Summer 2013

INTRODUCTION

Theresa May

Salmon Is Everything is a story about a watershed in crisis, a story intended to promote healing and change. Choctaw scholar LeAnne Howe argues that among Native peoles storytelling is understood as an action that can generate material change.[3] Stories are powerful forces of transformation, helping people remember and reclaim the past and call forth new visions of the future. At the heart of this book, and the play it contains, is a faith in the power of stories to build relationships, crack long-standing ideologies, open new possibilities, and reshape the social, political, and ecological landscapes of our lives.

The Klamath River begins in eastern Oregon, runs southwest, and enters the Pacific Ocean just south of the California-Oregon border. Forming the third largest watershed in the western United States, the Klamath is fed by eight major tributaries that support both human enterprise and wildlands in Oregon and California.[4] Like other great rivers of the West, the Klamath defies the borders and boundaries that govern civic life. Its main stem alone runs through five counties, as well as numerous irrigation districts, federally managed tracts of land, timber harvest areas, public recreation areas, national monuments, wildlife sanctuaries, and four federally recognized tribal areas—each with distinct languages and long-standing cultural relationships with the river. Klamath Falls, Oregon, with a population of twenty thousand, is the river's largest (and only) city. Along the Klamath's many tributaries and all along its winding path, small towns, unincorporated villages, private mines, farms, ranches, and homes thrive—but only if the river thrives.

The headwaters of the Klamath lie in a vast open plain of lakes and marshes fed by springs as well as by snowmelt from the eastern

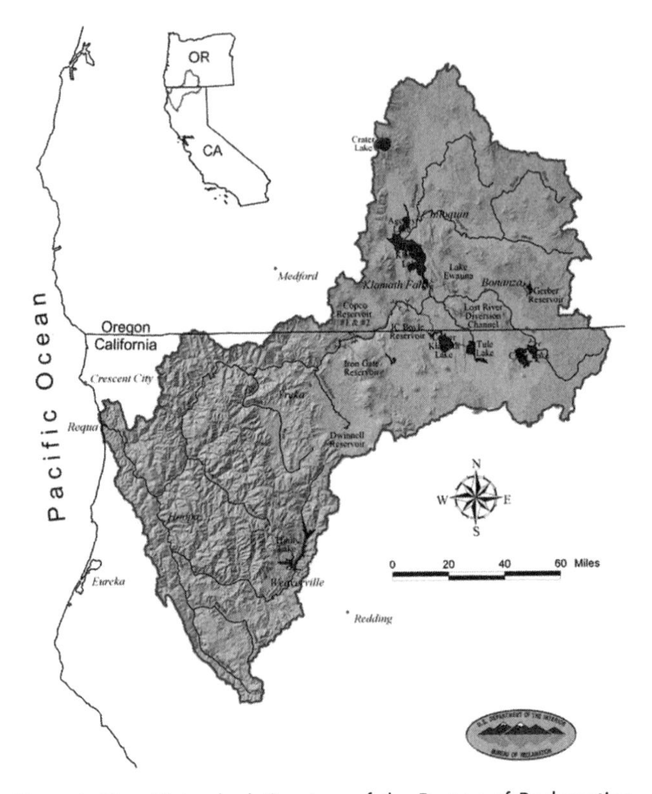

Klamath River Watershed. Courtesy of the Bureau of Reclamation, Klamath Falls.

Cascades. The three thousand square miles of the Upper Klamath, or Klamath Basin (for it holds the precious water that sustains life in the watershed), is bordered by Mount Thielsen and Crater Lake in the north and by Tule Lake and Lava Beds National Monument in the south. The Upper Klamath is the traditional homeland of the Klamath, Modoc, and Yahooskin peoples, who depended on the vast offerings of the marshlands and mountains for thousands of years before their first contact with Europeans. As Gordon Bettles writes in the foreword to this volume, the Upper Klamath has seen rapid change since the nineteenth-century arrival of settlers, who saw its expansive marshes as potential farmland. Under the treaty of 1864, the Klamath Tribes were to control the lands "from mountain top to mountain top." Yet Native stewardship of the land was in constant jeopardy as newcomers sought to capitalize on the region's rich farmland and abundant timber.

In 1906 the Klamath Project began selling federally owned land to farmers for agricultural development. Authorized under the 1902 Reclamation Act and managed by the Bureau of Reclamation, construction of several dams on the Klamath River would be funded with proceeds from homestead sales and would help provide project farmers with irrigation.[5] After World War I and World War II, veterans would receive priority for new homesteads. Meanwhile, the Klamath Termination Act of 1953 decimated tribal governance of its remaining lands, destroying the social and economic fabric of tribal life.[6] In the years that followed, agricultural and hydrological development of the region increased. The Klamath Project would impact the ecology of the river and its watershed well into the next century.[7]

At the Oregon-California border, where the Cascade Range, which runs north and south, collides with the Siskiyou Mountains, running east and west, the wide waters of the Klamath converge into a powerful singular flow. The water picks up speed and force as it crashes into canyons, pounds around geologic twists and turns, and cascades over sudden drops in elevation. The Mid-Klamath is rugged country and the ancestral homeland of the Karuk people, whose knowledge of the land has sustained them for thousands of years.[8] The Karuk fish the deep pools and rushing rapids of the river with traditional dip nets, bringing in harvests of salmon and steelhead that once made them the wealthiest tribe in California.[9] Downriver, near its confluence with the Trinity River, the Klamath flows through forests of cedar, Douglas-fir, and Sitka spruce, and the homeland of the Hupa people, who, like their Karuk neighbors, fish for salmon, hunt deer, elk, and other animals, and harvest a variety of plants. In northern California, where redwood-covered cliffs careen into the Pacific, the mouth of the Klamath River serves as a constant reminder to the Yurok people of the kinship between river and sea. Yurok homelands extend from the Pacific coast upriver to the Trinity confluence. In addition to hunting deer and elk, the Yurok harvest seaweed, abalone, mussels, and other foods from the Pacific shoreline and work the river's wide estuary for candlefish (smelt), eel, sturgeon, and salmon. Like the Karuk and Hupa, the Yurok have actively managed the land, river, and riparian zones in order to sustain these traditional foods for many generations.[10]

The Klamath is one of the great salmon spawning rivers of the Pacific Northwest, and Yurok elders remember a time when "the salmon were so plentiful you could walk across the river on their backs."[11] Chinook and coho salmon, along with steelhead trout, have returned to the mouth of the Klamath in fall and spring for millennia, part of one of the extraordinary migratory cycles on the planet. These anadromous fish sometimes swim hundreds of miles against the current, up rapids, over waterfalls, across lakes and human-made reservoirs, through irrigation culverts, and, if construction allows, around dams in order to return to their ancestral spawning grounds—streams, creeks, and tributaries throughout the Klamath watershed.[12] As demands on water resources, along with pollution and development, have compromised the health of rivers throughout the Pacific Northwest, populations of salmon have decreased. Salmon runs on the Klamath River have declined as much as 95 percent according to some estimates.[13] In the mid-1990s, the Klamath coho salmon was listed as threatened under the Endangered Species Act. In 2001 a

Thousands of dead and dying salmon washed up on the banks of the Klamath River during the fish kill of 2002. Photo: Northcoast Environmental Center.

drought in eastern Oregon precipitated a new battle in the region's water wars as farmers and ranchers demanded that agriculture take priority over fish. Then, in September of 2002, just as thousands of coho and chinook salmon were beginning their long journey home, upward of thirty-four thousand died prematurely, leaving thousands of salmon corpses floating and putrefying along miles of riverbank.[14]

News of the die-off, or "fish kill," spread through north coast communities like wildfire. The deaths of so many salmon threw a national spotlight on the decades-long conflict over water use along the Oregon-California border. I was in my first year of teaching at Humboldt State University in Arcata, California, about sixty miles south of the mouth of the Klamath River—the site of the carnage. In response to the fish kill, university president Rollin Richmond hosted a conference on Klamath River water policy, inviting scientists and representatives from state, federal, and regional government agencies dealing with water, land management, and wildlife, as well as citizen and environmental groups and local tribal leaders to discuss the underlying causes and to advocate plans of action. I attended the conference in order to learn more about what had happened and why. The room was electric with antagonisms, palpable through the veil of professional presentations, revealing that the issues of water rights and allocation, species protection, human economies, and cultural rights are thick with layers of contested history. As I listened, I could not help but notice that the back of the room was crowded with people from the tribal communities, for whom the catastrophe was not only economic (with measurable loss for tribal fisheries that season) but also cultural, spiritual, and personal. For Native people, a threat to salmon was a threat to traditional ways of life. As scientists and government officials presented their theories, Native elders sat silent, as if keeping vigil at the proceedings. No one invited them to speak, at least not in the sessions I attended.

I began to think about the voices in the larger story that were not being heard, and how I might use my position of power and privilege as an academic and an artist to help amplify those voices. I came to Humboldt State after a decade as an arts educator in the Seattle area, where I had developed programs that taught ecological values and environmental education through the performing arts. I wrote plays with students and communities on non–point source pollution, salmon habitat restoration, and watershed history. Listening to the presentations that afternoon, I began to think about a play as a way to tell the story of what was a profoundly personal trauma for my Yurok, Karuk, and Hupa neighbors. Stories, I thought, might make the kind of difference that more data and debate might not, particularly when shared in a forum where judgments are temporarily suspended, as they are in the theatre. As a result of what I had seen and heard at the conference, I was particularly interested in structuring a project that gave space to the experiences and viewpoints of those who shared a direct subsistence relationship with the salmon, and whose voices and suffering seemed to be little acknowledged in the calamity of September 2002.

Those voices are essential to balanced civic discourse. In "Communication and the Other: Beyond Deliberative Democracy," Iris Marion Young provides a distinction that sheds fresh light on the function of diversity in democracy. Like most of us, I was accustomed to what Young calls "deliberative democracy," in which positions are laid out through debate, and decisions made by majority voices. Under this deliberative model, difference is something to be transcended, something to be worked through in order to find "common ground."[15] But deliberative democracy's quest for agreement, Young argues, may merely reinscribe privilege by dismissing knowledge represented by the experience of marginalized groups precisely because it is not commonly held (such as the Yurok belief that the Salmon are spirit beings and brothers as well as sustenance). Young notes that the "problem with this conception of the unity of democratic discussion is that it may harbor another mechanism of exclusion . . . where some groups have greater symbolic or material privilege than others." The Klamath watershed is typical of the pluralist body politic Young describes, one that "face[s] serious divergences in value premises, cultural practices and meanings." Among the water users of the Klamath River, ranchers and farmers count themselves as the contemporary counterparts of pioneer Americans, and their economic needs carry a symbolic privilege that has ensured political advantage. In these circumstances, Young observes, the hurried quest to find agreement can drown out marginalized voices by privileging "the dispassionate, the educated, or those who feel they have a right to assert." Young argues instead for a "communicative democracy" in which difference is valued and disagreement becomes a source of new knowledge. In communicative democracy "each can tell her story with equal authority," allowing the community to access its "total social knowledge." Young's distinction carves out an important democratic function for theatre and the arts in general—as forums where stories, and the wisdom and knowledge they carry, are given authority. Stories preserve and disseminate wisdom, provide historical context, and transmit feelings that have the power to change the listener, easing long-standing social and political polarization.

Over a three-year period, I worked closely with Native faculty, staff, students, and community members throughout the Klamath watershed to research and write a play that told the story of people directly affected by the river's crisis—we called this the Klamath Theatre Project (KTP). This volume includes the full text of its culmination—*Salmon Is Everything*—as well as reflections on its development process. In compiling this volume, we have worked against the expectation of a single authorial voice, opting instead for a structure similar to the play—one that is multivocal and episodic—in order to demonstrate how artists, academics, and communities might work together to tell stories that need to be told. The Klamath Theatre Project was a learning adventure for everyone involved, not unlike a white-water rafting trip down one of the Klamath's many tributaries: everyone paddles, everyone gets wet, and everyone learns how dependent we are on one another, and on the river.

The volume begins with Suzanne Burcell's "A Call to Action: We Have to Do Something!" in which she writes about the Karuk people's understanding of kinship with salmon. Suzanne was director of the Indian Teacher and Educational Personnel Program at Humboldt State and a primary collaborator and adviser throughout the project. She also describes the process of developing consensus about the purpose of the project, and its reception by the Native community when finally performed on stage.

The text of *Salmon Is Everything* follows, with complete production information. The play is an example of the ways in which story, memory, ceremony, prayer, and imagery are part of what Young calls "the situated knowledge available . . . and the combination of narratives from different perspectives [that] produce the collective wisdom not available from any one position." The aim of *Salmon Is Everything* is a change of heart. It is meant as a celebration of multiple voices, experience, and knowledge within our watershed community.

In "I Am Karuk! My Voice as Rose," Kathleen McCovey describes her experience as a collaborator and member of the acting ensemble. She originated the role of Rose, and her voice reverberates through the play. As a Karuk elder, Indigenous environmentalist, and community leader, Kathleen writes about how working on and performing in the play influenced her work as a spokesperson for her tribe. Her story illuminates the potential for theatre to support and strengthen individual voices. This second edition includes a new reflection by Marta Lu Clifford, who played the role of Rose at the University of Oregon. Marta's "Becoming Rose" provides a window into her experience and the potential theatre has to amplify Native voices around important issues of environmental justice and tribal sovereignty.

In "The Education of an Artist," I map my journey as a non-Native artist and educator working in collaboration with Native and non-Native students, colleagues, and community members. I have tried to be candid about the many challenges, surprises, confusions, awkward moments, and new understandings that were part of my education as an "outsider." Challenges including questions of authority, ownership of stories, creative license, interpretation, voice, inclusion, and cultural protocol were learning opportunities for me and for everyone involved.

We embarked on rehearsals of the play-in-progress in autumn 2005, aiming for a first production in spring 2006, and I asked my theatre colleague and friend Jean O'Hara to codirect. (Jean's partner, Jessica Eden, had been part of the KTP collaborative group, and the characters of Kate and Rachel are based in part on their experience as a queer identified couple living in a rural community.) Following the production, Jean and members of the ensemble took *Salmon Is Everything* on tour to communities along the Klamath River. In "The Journey Home," Jean describes the challenges of taking the play "home."

This second edition includes a new chapter, "Story, Sovereignty, Relationality, and Place: Teaching *Salmon Is Everything*," by Kirby Brown, professor of Native Studies at the University of Oregon. Motivated by the protests at Standing Rock, he describes teaching the play in the context of a course about cultural production and stories of place in indigenous environmental movements. He describes how he centered the importance of place and coming into relation in the process of student consciousness-raising.

In the spring of 2006, just as we produced the play for the first time, I accepted a position at the University of Oregon. I hoped that the Klamath Theatre Project would continue on in my absence, but it did not. My decision to change institutions deepened my appreciation of the ways in which Native people are connected to place, and it set my outsider status in relief once more: I could come and go. Kathleen McCovey reminded me at the time that Native people are connected to the land through kinship—a bond she could not break for the sake of a job opportunity. At the University of Oregon I met Gordon Bettles, the director of the university's Many Nations Longhouse and a member of the Klamath Tribes, and my bond with the Klamath River and the play was renewed. Conversations with Gordon led to a production of *Salmon Is Everything* at the University of Oregon in spring 2011. In the process, the play was revised to reflect a stronger Klamath-Modoc perspective, and that is the version printed here.

One of the challenges of community-based theatre is crediting those whose voices were part of its creation. As I began writing and weaving the text of the play, drawing on the research and reflective writing of students and community members, as well as myself, I became increasingly uncomfortable with the ways in which many community-based plays are published—giving the playwright authorship even though the stories emerged from the community. Story is a deeply respected form of knowledge for the Native people with whom I worked, and Native people know too well the ways their traditional stories have been appropriated and commodified. It is important to say here, then, that each person whose contribution became part of *Salmon Is Everything* remains the owner of his or her own stories and words. Those words and stories are loaned in trust, not unlike a land trust, and must be tended and respected for their intent. With *Salmon Is Everything* we are proposing a new model for crediting community-based texts: the play is annotated with footnotes to identify the person whose words or research became passages in the play.[16] The title of the play is taken from Barry McCovey Jr.'s description of the salmon's central place in tribal life.[17] An archive of the Klamath Theatre Project can be found in the special collections of Humboldt State University Library.[18]

The authors of the chapters in this book, as well as the characters in the play itself, use a variety of words to identify themselves and their neighbors as Indigenous People of the Klamath Watershed. As Michael Yellow Bird reminds us, words matter precisely because they have been used to hurt people.[19] Language can perpetuate stereotypes, erase cultures, and silence or misrepresent others. Language is loaded with the legacies of colonialization and is instrumental in ongoing colonialism today. Words themselves often carry the persistent patterns of that shared history. "Indian" and "Native American" are, after all, the colonizer's names for the diverse Indigenous Peoples of this continent. In this book the specific name of a tribe or tribes is used when the meaning or context allows; "Native" is used when speaking generally, and "Indigenous Peoples" when the context suggests a larger geopolitical frame that ties local struggles to pan-indigenous struggles for sovereignty. The term "Indian" is used by government agencies and so occurs as part of those legal designations. It may also be integral to a quote, or necessary for meaning. Language is always about sovereignty and self-determination, and allowing people to decide how they wish to refer to themselves is paramount. Authors of the chapters use words that they have chosen to talk about themselves, their community, and history. Characters in the play use a variety of terms. As voices developed from interviews and informal conversations of everyday life, characters reflect the dynamic and complicated ways that change affects language. Sometimes a character will use several different terms, even in one scene. For example, Tim, who is struggling to become a more effective ally, uses "Indian," which may seem insensitive to the very community he wants to support. Yet, he also uses tribe-specific names, indicating perhaps that he is engaged in a dynamic learning process that includes decolonizing his own speech. Andy, a Karuk professor of biology, refers to his tribal name, but also uses "Indian" and "Native," as he reflects in the Town Hall on the cultural biases that have ignored the ways in which Karuk people have always tended the land. The reader is encouraged to consider how language reflects each character's history and experiences. In every case, context and intention are key to unpacking the shifting use and meaning of words. Who is speaking? In what situation and to whom? What is their intention? The complex personal and political implications of an author's or character's use of one term or another can be a seed-starter for talking about why and how language reflects the legacies of history, and how people are taking back, renewing, and reclaiming language.

Plays are civic documents that record the human sensibilities and experiences of a particular historical moment. Through the magic of theatre, the past lives with and through the present, just as the 2002 fish kill still lives in the present for Native people of the Klamath River. The threat of future loss of salmon species and culture continues as long as the river bears the weight of its several dams. As an archive of collective memory, *Salmon Is Everything* marks several turning points in the politics of the Klamath watershed. It premiered in 2006 in the wake of a tragedy and the heat of a public debate. By the time the play was staged at the University of Oregon in 2011, the ground had shifted, and the Klamath communities were talking seriously about dam removal. As this second edition goes to press, hopes are high for the deconstruction of four dams and restoration of salmon runs. Farmers, ranchers, and the general public have come to better understand and appreciate the significance of salmon populations to Indigenous cultures as well as ecosystem health. Meanwhile, the dams have ceased to make economic sense for the corporations that own and operate them. In September 2009, Klamath watershed stakeholders reached two historic agreements designed to lead to the removal of four dams, the restoration of water flow for fish, as well as allocations of water for farmers: the Klamath Basin Restoration Agreement and the Klamath Hydroelectric Settlement Agreement. Some argued that these agreements did not guarantee adequate water for the salmon during drought years, while others claimed that landowners would be deprived of their property rights. Nevertheless, the agreements were heralded by the *New York Times* on February 9, 2010, as a "stunning example of how cooperation and partnership can resolve difficult conflicts." But the provisions of the Klamath agreements required federal funding, and as the first edition of *Salmon Is Everything* went to press in 2014, bills that would authorize that funding languished in Congress. Despite extensions, the agreements expired on December 31, 2014.

"But Salmon People are used to swimming upstream," an elder told me. Watershed residents would do it themselves. The Karuk and Yurok, together with other tribes and allies in the Klamath watershed, continued to pursue the goal of dam removal and salmon restoration without the support of the federal government. The approaching mandate for PacifiCorp to relicense the dams has suggested a window of opportunity. None of the four dams proposed for removal in the earlier agreements provided irrigation or drinking water, but all were responsible for decreased flows for downriver salmon habitat. Between 2011 and 2014 California and Oregon continued to experience severe drought, exacerbating impacts on salmon and the subsistence communities and commercial fisheries that depend on them. Under the Federal Energy Regulatory Commission (FERC) relicensing would require PacifiCorp to make repairs and improvements (including fish ladders) to continue operations. As it became clear to PacifiCorp and its holding company, Berkshire Hathaway, that the cost of relicensing dams was greater than the revenues the dams generated in hydropower, the company became increasingly willing to negotiate with river stakeholders. In 2016 PacifiCorp/Berkshire Energy agreed to surrender the dams as part of the regular FERC procedures. Meanwhile, the Karuk Tribe, along with other stakeholders to the Klamath agreements of 2010, formed the Klamath River Renewal Corporation, a 501(c)3 nonprofit corporation that would take ownership of the four dams and carry out the project of dam removal. Funding would come partly from PacifiCorp (at less than the cost of relicensing, plus releasing them from liability), and partly from a 2014 California water bond, Proposition 1. No federal funds required. The new KRRC is a dynamic example of tribal sovereignty, civic tenacity, and common sense working toward a more just and sustainable future. The next step is FERC approval of the plan to surrender and transfer the four dams. But regulatory normalcy has deteriorated in the new political climate in Washington, DC. The five-member commission currently has two members, with three to be appointed by the current administration. FERC cannot make a decision without a quorum. As we goes to press the plan to decommission and deconstruct the dams by 2020 is on hold yet again.[20]

It was a critical time for the Klamath watershed when this play was developed, and the first edition of this book expressed our hope that the 2010 Klamath agreements would be funded. Eight years later, urgency deepens and *Salmon Is Everything* helps us remember the consequences of our collective choices. This second edition goes to press with a prayer: that the residents of the Klamath watershed make choices that strengthen community and that the Klamath River is wild and free by 2020.

In the reflective essays included here, each author writes in narrative style from their best and individual recollection. We are only a few voices from a collaborative effort that included dozens of people, each of whom has a unique story. We have tried to represent our fellow collaborators honorably. We hope the process of developing *Salmon Is Everything* provides a model for how the arts can open a space for multiple and underrepresented viewpoints and contribute to healing historical trauma. We believe that the empathy that emerges from reading, participating in, or witnessing a community-based performance such as this can lead to deeper, more complex understandings, form new relationships across cultural and racial differences, and lay the groundwork for compassionate civic action.

A CALL TO ACTION

We Have to *Do* Something!

Suzanne M. Burcell

For thousands of years before contact with non-Indigenous people, the Karuk-arara, or "Upriver People," made their homes in more than one hundred villages along the Upper Klamath River in the heavily forested, mountainous regions of northwestern California now known as Siskiyou and Humboldt Counties. Our aboriginal territory encompasses more than a million acres of land traversed by the Klamath and Salmon Rivers and many streams and tributaries, where the salmon, steelhead, elk, deer, ducks, geese, grouse, quail, tan oak acorns, and a variety of seasonal berries, mushrooms, and roots once provided sustenance in a lush natural environment. Throughout history the Karuk and neighboring tribal peoples have been well recognized as fishers, hunters, and gatherers; weavers of fine-twilled baskets; and makers of redwood dugout canoes, split cedar houses, and beautiful dance regalia. We continue to be singers, dancers, and traditional healers whose ceremonies celebrate the return of the salmon, "fix the earth" by restoring balance, and renew the world for harmonious living.

For the Karuk people, whose native language is of the Hokan family, the center of the universe is at Katimiin, near the confluence of the Salmon and Klamath Rivers. Neighboring tribes in Humboldt County include the Yurok, of the Algonquian language family, who are indigenous to the Lower Klamath River region; and the Hupa, of the Athabascan language family and Trinity River, which flows into the Klamath about twenty-five miles downriver from Katimiin. Although our languages are very different, the Karuk, Yurok, and Hupa peoples have many traditions in common. Historically, we traded material goods, and today we continue to marry intertribally and participate in each other's ceremonies.

In the 1850s the traditional village lifestyles, subsistence economies, and intertribal trade networks of the Karuk people and neighboring tribes ended suddenly and violently with the California gold rush. As miners moved into northern California to stake their claims—and as the US Cavalry followed to ensure their safety—Karuk and other tribal peoples were murdered, massacred, and enslaved. Whole villages were burned, and the life-giving Klamath River watershed was damaged forever by hydraulic mining and mercury contamination. Many of the tribal peoples who survived the immediate impacts of the gold rush moved away in search of alternative means of survival. During the late 1800s and early 1900s, children of the tribal peoples who remained in their aboriginal territories were forcibly removed from their families and sent to government boarding schools in Oregon, Nevada, southern California, and even more distant places. There they were expected to learn the language, mannerisms, religious beliefs, and vocational trades of the encroaching populations.

For 140 years, the economy of the region continued to be natural resource driven; gold and copper mining soon were followed by the timber industry, which peaked in the mid-1900s, declined in the 1970s and 1980s, and ultimately was curtailed in the early 1990s, except on the Hoopa Valley and Yurok Reservations, where the tribes manage forestlands on a sustained yield basis. Today the Klamath and Trinity River region—for thousands of years a tranquil system of family villages and for another century dotted with boomtowns of miners and loggers—remains unhealed from the devastating effects of two major disruptions of social and economic systems. The earth has been ravaged by mining and clear-cutting; the salmon spawning grounds degraded by soil erosion and sedimentation; the deer, elk, and other wild game populations decimated; and we, the surviving tribal peoples, face the daunting challenge of restoring and renewing our homelands for future generations.

Among the tribal elders, elected leaders, and general memberships of the Hoopa Valley, Karuk, and Yurok Tribes, there is perhaps no stronger sense of purpose, no stronger point of consensus, than the shared responsibility for land stewardship—all three tribal governments have worked long and hard to regain decision-making authority over tribal lands, watersheds, and wildlife habitats so that those resources might be protected by the teachings of our elders, passed from generation to generation, and increasingly managed by the integration of Native values and worldviews, intrinsic knowledge of natural history, and growing bodies of scientific knowledge about ecology and environmental restoration. The Hoopa Valley, Karuk, and Yurok Tribes (self-governance or "compact" tribes under Public Law 93-638) employ professional fisheries and wildlife biologists and technicians, foresters and silviculturists, air and water quality monitoring technicians, wildfire protection crews, forest fuels reduction crews, and GIS specialists, as well as political analysts and self-governance policy advocates, to ensure that the tribes' environmental protection efforts are well supported in all legal and political jurisdictional arenas. Until the fall of 2002, there was a generally hopeful (albeit tenuous) sense that the local tribes' combined efforts were having beneficial influences on the various federal and state agencies with which they shared responsibility for environmental protection on Indian lands.

And then something unimaginably horrific happened—something of such overwhelming magnitude it left whole communities of people, tribal and nontribal, shocked, heartsick, spiritually devastated. In late September 2002, we began to hear reports that hundreds, possibly thousands, of dead salmon were washing up along the banks of the Lower Klamath River. One of the most vivid reports I read was an article in *Indian Country Today* entitled "Fish Kill: For the Yurok, Salmon Is Everything." It was written by twenty-four-year-old Barry McCovey Jr., a Yurok fisheries technician whose distress was palpable.

> As a Yurok Tribal member and college student in the fisheries field, I spend my days working along the Klamath. The carnage I've seen over the past week and a half is so utterly grotesque

> that I cannot sleep at night. I close my eyes and the images of dead, rotting fish envelop me. You may have seen photographs in newspapers or caught a glimpse on the television, but you cannot begin to imagine the smell. This smell of death and decay is impossible to escape. It fills the air and plays with the mind in ways that I could never describe. I can't eat because food, no matter what it is, reminds me of the smell. Perhaps it's because the rotting fish represent so much of my people's food gone to waste. The water levels in the river have never been in such decline. Numerous tribal and non-tribal elders have assured me of this fact. In my lifetime, I have never seen the Klamath so shallow. (October 4, 2002)

For those driven by such inconceivable reports to go and see for themselves, this unprecedented event would be profoundly life changing. One of them was my Yurok niece, a public schoolteacher in the town of Hoopa, who also was working on her master's degree at Humboldt State University, where I served as director of the Indian Teacher and Educational Personnel Program (ITEPP; later the name was changed to the Indian Tribal and Educational Personnel Program). She came to me with her photographs of dead and rotting fish—hundreds and hundreds of them—their bodies blown or torn open, lying along the Klamath River's edge near the ceremonial grounds where just weeks earlier the salmon had been central to our tribal dances. Tearfully, she turned the pages of her photo album, alternately asking "How could this happen?" and answering her own question: "We have to *do* something—we can't let this happen again—we *have* to do *some*thing." Ultimately she withdrew from graduate school in order to devote more time to community-based environmental activism.

As the days of fall passed, and the dead fish counts grew to "more than 30,000" and "potentially twice that many," the emotional distress of tribal students and staff on campus grew more and more pronounced. Shock gave way to anger—who was to blame for this obviously unnatural disaster? Our tribes were doing everything they could to protect "all our relations"—all living things—and certainly the salmon fisheries were of highest priority among all the tribes. Slowly came information about a parasite (ich) and bacterial pathogen (columnaris) blamed for the fish kill, but it made little sense to anyone that these commonly occurring threats had suddenly killed fifty thousand or more salmon.[21]

What were we not being told? Suspicions grew as rumors surfaced about the suppression of federal biologists' reports that forewarned that the volume of Klamath River flows being diverted to alleviate drought conditions on Oregon farms would result in a major fish kill downriver. Slowly it began to sink in that the fish kill had been preventable—and the real answer had more to do with politics (namely, electoral votes generated by Oregon-based farmers) than good science or fisheries management.

Now came the outrage—triggered by a level of pain that pierced the hearts of our people. A century and a half after the massacres and environmental destruction of the California gold rush era—and the subsequent social, political, and environmental healing efforts of our tribes notwithstanding—the federal government had willfully sacrificed our primary source of sustenance for the economic gains of Oregon farmers and the expected political gains of their votes in the 2004 presidential election! In one incredibly shortsighted and self-serving move, the Bush-Cheney administration had pitted non-Native and Native American citizens against each other, resurrecting the nineteenth-century doctrine of Manifest Destiny, and ripping open the still unhealed wounds inflicted by a national legacy of cultural genocide. I couldn't help thinking, "Really? Are we really right back to a 'cowboys and Indians' mentality?" I felt betrayed (perhaps naively so) and utterly alienated from the general populace of this country.

"So what," I asked myself, "would be 'right action' for me, Sue Burcell, taught by my father and grandfather I could always return to Katimiin for physical and spiritual sustenance?" What were my appropriate roles as a member of the Karuk Tribe, as director of a university-based Indian education program, and as a teacher of the history of Indian education, a course that chronicled the early history of genocide of North American tribal peoples, as well as our improved social, political, and economic conditions under slowly evolving federal Indian laws, including the Indian Self-Determination and Education Assistance Act? Could I continue to do this work without compromising my integrity? Was the 2002 fish kill a harbinger of things to come, or a fluke of some kind to which we should react forcefully but (somehow) strategically? It was hard to imagine, given the overwhelming sense of loss that pervaded our students, families, and communities, what might constitute an overreaction. I prayed.

Within a short time (days or weeks, I don't remember), a diminutive and soft-spoken woman visited my ITEPP office and introduced herself as Theresa May, a new member of the Theatre Arts faculty, who had heard about the Klamath River fish kill and had some ideas that might help. She asked if I had heard of "ecodrama," indicating she had had some success with it as a way of raising public awareness of environmental issues and facilitating dialogues that illuminated diverse perspectives. As I sat pondering the possibility that a better-informed general public—one that understood, even appreciated, different points of view—might be essential to a strategic response, Theresa asked directly, "Do you think some of your students might be interested in working with a group of Theatre Arts students to explore the issues underlying the salmon kill? I don't think it can be done without involving Native students, and I don't think we have any in Theatre Arts." She seemed earnest, and I honestly had no better idea what to do at a time when something needed to be done. (One of life's important lessons is that prayers can be answered in unexpected ways.)

After a moment, I said, "I don't know whether our students would be interested or not, but our student services coordinator, Phil Zastrow, advises students about their course schedules—and he's involved in local community theatre. Let's see what he thinks. If students *are* interested, I could offer American Indian Education (AIE) course credits for their participation."

We proceeded to Phil's office, and by spring of 2003, a diverse group of Humboldt State students were enrolled in concurrent, special-topic "Klamath Theatre Project" courses in AIE, Native American Studies, and Theatre Arts. It was the beginning of a three-year process of collaborative research, script development, casting, and dramatic production—as well as personal self-discovery. Students amassed volumes of public and tribal news stories and government reports. They interviewed tribal elders, leaders, and fisheries biologists. They engaged in lively discussions in ITEPP's kitchen, living room, and Curriculum Resource Center—with a seriousness of purpose I had not witnessed before the salmon kill—and they exemplified ITEPP's mission: "to promote Indian self-determination by creating learning communities that validate Tribal cultural values, facilitate academic success, and foster a sense of self-efficacy among American Indian students, educators, and professionals." It felt good—it felt *right*—it felt like *righteous* work was being done!

By the third semester, as Theresa and her students wove tribal perspectives on the Klamath River, salmon fisheries, and related environmental issues into a script for an ecodrama, they began to do introductory readings at educational, social, and environmental justice summits on and off campus. With each reading and follow-on discussion, audience members shared new firsthand accounts; many of them were integrated into the evolving script. It was going well, and the students' staid accountability to family and friends in our river communities reinforced their growing belief that this *was* in fact important work—our people *would* be heard—it was real and validating and at times exhausting.

Then came a day when a small group of ITEPP students entered my office, obviously upset and unsure they wanted to continue working with Theresa. "She wants us to include the perspective of the farmers!" they exclaimed. One young woman added, "I don't even *want* to understand the farmers' perspective—it feels like a betrayal of my own people to even *try* to go there! Do we have to do this?"

This question is key, I thought, as I heard myself say, "Yes, I think we do—if no one wants to understand the perspective of anyone else, how will issues as complex as these ever get resolved? Unless the play includes fair representations of *all* the stakeholders, we won't gain any ground—instead of just being *right* (which everyone thinks they are), we need to be mutually respectful. We can do that without betraying our own beliefs, our own people." The stunned students stared at me in disbelief, looked at each other to see whether they had all heard the same thing, and left without responding. I honestly didn't know whether they would continue working on the play. Had I said the wrong thing—or said it too quickly? Once more I prayed.

Toward the end of the second year, Theresa May asked me to read the near-final script. She said, "I think we've captured the perspectives of most of the stakeholders—tribal peoples, farmers, ranchers, environmentalists, government agencies, even the news media—can you think of anyone else?"

"What about the fish?" I asked.

"The fish?" Theresa's eyes widened.

"The fish," I said again. "It occurs to me that in all of this discussion about the fish *kill*, the perspective of the fish *themselves* is lost. I mean, the fish are living, breathing, and life giving—part of Creation, and procreation. What if you were one of these beautiful salmon, just trying to swim upriver, to return to your birthplace and spawn? Isn't that what this whole drama is about—reverence for life?"

"Well, how would we portray the perspective of the fish in the play?" Theresa asked.

"There's a group based in Orleans that has been filming salmon underwater for some time now—they heard about our ecodrama and called me. They offered to contribute film footage to the production. I think it would be the perfect backdrop for the play—fish being fish, as Creator intended them to be." We requested the footage, which provided unforgettable imagery of underwater life and, together with the naturally musical sounds of flowing water, took the viewing audience beyond just seeing and hearing the play to experiencing its core messages in appropriately visceral ways.

When at last it was time to hold auditions for the *Salmon Is Everything* cast, one thing was clear: the roles of tribal characters would be played by tribal people. A call went out from the university's Theatre Arts Department and Native student programs for interested students and community members (with or without acting experience) to audition for the play. Some of the students from classes that had researched and developed essential content for the script responded to the call, as did some of the students, staff, and faculty who had participated in earlier script readings. Others, especially community members who had contributed from the audiences at various readings, were sought out and persuaded that their authenticity in central roles would be at least as convincing as acting talent. This was their story—no one could tell it better, no one would have a better chance of being *heard*, than they.

One by one, a cast of familiar faces came together, at first tenuously, but with each rehearsal growing more confident in their abilities to perform, and stronger in their personal convictions about the importance of this undertaking. Several actors (and parents of actors) traveled more than a hundred miles a day (at their own expense) for months of rehearsals on the Humboldt State campus. I shall not forget the night my grandson Ish-Kaysh returned from a particularly long rehearsal, found me in the kitchen, and reported in an unusually solemn nine-year-old voice, "Grandma, this play that we're doing is important—I mean, it's *really important* to Indian people."

In May of 2006, three years after the Klamath Theatre Project began, *Salmon Is Everything* premiered in the university's Studio Theatre, a small "black box" facility with seating for approximately 150 people. A day before the public premiere, there was a special performance for tribal elders, performers' families and friends, and other community members. As I entered the building, a wave of anxiety swept over me. It suddenly struck me there was a lot at stake here—and, having avoided the last rehearsals so I could experience the play as it was meant to be, I had no idea how it might be received. My apprehension subsided when I saw codirector Jean O'Hara just inside the entrance, smiling as she welcomed the community. "Keep the faith," I counseled myself, as I took a seat inside the theatre.

For the next ninety minutes, I was so thoroughly immersed in *Salmon Is Everything* that I had little awareness of the audience at all. To my relief, the theatrical production did not *over*dramatize—instead, it reminded me of the traditional storytelling I experienced in my childhood. The messages were clear and compelling, poignant and at times profoundly sad, but also balanced in perspective and emotion, with appropriately humorous moments. I felt an almost instant affinity with each character—leaving so little room for polarizing judgments that empathy came easily as we sat silently taking it all in. Just once I allowed myself to scan the audience, noticing only their intent watching and listening, and an occasional affirming nod from an elder.

We were witnessing something extraordinary—something so revealing and emotionally engaging it took us a few minutes to disengage after the play ended. And then came the applause that slowly grew into a standing ovation. Over the mounting sounds of clapping and whistling, a young man's voice rose, shouting, "Yes, yes! This is what we need! This is a *lot* better than those fish council meetings with everybody screaming across the table at everybody else! *This* is what we need! More of this!" I wondered if he had any idea how gratifying that validation—and the escalating cheers it prompted—must have been to my friends, Theresa May and Jean O'Hara, to Kathy McCovey, Margaret Mary Campbell, Jason Reed (and his father Ron Reed), Robin Andrews, Darcie Breeman-Black, Mack Owen, Josephine Johnson, and to young Mary Risling and Ish-Kaysh Tripp (and their beaming families)—and to all the others who had worked so long and hard on this production.

For some of us, it was a life-affirming moment. A way had been found to inform, to facilitate meaningful and mutually respectful dialogue, to bridge cultures, and to begin a long-awaited healing process. I gave thanks.

SALMON IS EVERYTHING

A Community-Based Play from the Klamath Watershed

THERESA MAY AND THE KLAMATH THEATRE PROJECT

Salmon Is Everything was developed in collaboration with students, faculty, staff, and community members who believe that by sharing stories we can grow the compassion necessary for change, justice, and ecological sustainability. We have called ourselves the Klamath Theatre Project. The characters are fictional composites meant to represent the various constituencies of the Klamath River watershed and are not intended to represent specific individuals. Small parts of the play are drawn from previously published work. Scenes 2 and 15 are drawn, in part, from "Fish Kill: For the Yurok, Salmon Is Everything" by Barry McCovey Jr.; and portions of scenes 3, 17, and 19 are adapted from "Yainix Journal" by Becky Hatfield Hyde. These sources are noted in the play as well as in the bibliography.

For information about producing *Salmon Is Everything*, contact Theresa May at the University of Oregon, Eugene, Oregon 97403, or the publisher of this volume.

Klamath Theatre Project collaborators included: Heather Hostler, Lauren Taylor, Nikolai Colegrove, Jessica Eden, Ron Griffith, Christina Perez, Aaron Waxman, Kendall Allen, Holly Couling, Roberta Chavez, Nicole Barchilon Frank, Jean O'Hara, Marlon and Dale Sherman, Phil Zastrow, Ron Reed, Mary Campbell, Suzanne Burcell, Kathleen McCovey, Bryan Colegrove, Robin Andrews, Darcie Beeman-Black, Jacob Froneberger, Beth Weissbart, Talia Sophia Moss, Ethan Frank, Bubba (Glen) Sanchez, Arianna McLennan, Judy Risling, Mary Risling, Marlette Grant-Jackson, Ish-Kaysh Tripp, Katie Skinner, and Nora Chatmon. Contributions to revisions for the 2011 production came from Gordon Bettles, Tom Ball, James Florendo, Kevin Simmons, Derek Kimbol, Badger Kimbol, Delia Sanchez, Ariana Sanchez, Perri McDaniel, Adriana Wahwahsuck, Diana Ortero, Ahavah Oblak, Raffi Halevy, Shayleen Macy, Jules Bacon, Ada Ball, Richie Scott, Marta Clifford, Kunu Dittmer, Ted Vasquez, and the cast and production team.

PRODUCTION HISTORY:

Salmon Is Everything was presented at Humboldt State University in May 2006, directed by Theresa May and Jean O'Hara; cultural advisers, Kathleen McCovey and Suzanne Burcell; set designer, Lila Nelson; lighting designer, Emily Blanche; film montage, Christa Dickman; images courtesy of the Klamath Restoration Council and Michael Hentz. The cast was as follows:

JULIE .... Mary Campbell
WILL, MIDRIVER MAN .... Jason Reed
ROSE .... Kathleen McCovey
JOHNNY, MODOC MAN .... Bobbie Perez
LOUISE, LOWER KLAMATH WOMAN .... Robin Andrews
LITTLE MARY .... Mary Risling
ZEEK .... Ethan Frank
KATE .... Darcie Beeman-Black
RACHEL, FEMALE TOURIST, WHITE-WATER GUIDE .... Beth Weissbart
ALICE, FISHERIES WOMAN .... Josephine Johnson
TIM .... Lincoln Mitchell
GRACE .... Talia Sophia Moss
REPORTER .... Jacob Froneberger
ANDY .... Phil Zastrow
MAX, PHILLIP .... Marlon Sherman
MALE TOURIST, WALT, PRIEST .... Jason Tower
VOICEOVERS .... Kendall Allen, Roberta Chavez

A touring production of *Salmon Is Everything* was presented in various locations on the Klamath River in summer 2007, directed by Jean O'Hara; production assistant, Jennifer Burgess. The cast was as follows:

JULIE .... Mary Campbell
ROSE .... Kathleen McCovey
WILL, MIDRIVER MAN, MODOC MAN .... Bubba (Glen) Sanchez
LOIUSE, LOWER KLAMATH WOMAN .... Arianna McLennan
LITTLE MARY .... Mary Risling

ZEEK .... Ish-Kaysh Tripp
KATE .... Darcie Beeman-Black
RACHEL, FEMALE TOURIST, ALICE, FISHERIES WOMAN .... Judy Sears
TIM .... Lincoln Mitchell
GRACE .... Talia Sophia Moss
REPORTER .... Nora Chatmon
MAX, PHILLIP, ANDY .... Phil Zastrow
WHITE-WATER GUIDE .... Katie Skinner
MALE TOURIST, WALT, PRIEST .... Jason Tower

Salmon Is Everything was presented by the University of Oregon in May 2011, directed by Theresa May; cultural advisers, Gordon Bettles and James Florendo; dramaturge, Jules Bacon; set designer, Dan Carlgren; costume designer, Gina Love; lighting designer, Jarvis Jahner; choreographers, James Florendo and Piper Ruiz; stage manager, Hallie Day. The cast was as follows:

JULIE .... Shayleen Macy EagleSpeaker
ROSE .... Marta Lu Clifford
WILL .... Kunu Dittmer
JOHNNY , KLAMATH TRIBAL MEMBER .... Richie Scott
LOUISE .... Ada Ball
LITTLE MARY .... Diana Ortero and Ariana Sanchez
ZEEK .... Badger Kimbol and Sunil Holmes
KATE .... Sarah Ruggles
RACHEL .... Hannah Hogan
TIM .... Martin Diaz-Valdes
ALICE .... Jean Sidden
BEN .... Rafael Halevy
REPORTER .... Piper Ruiz
ANDY, PHILLIP .... Ted Vasquez
POLITICIAN, WOMAN TOURIST .... Christine Madzik
WALT, MALE TOURIST .... Joseph Gilg
LOGGER'S DAUGHTER .... Chelsea Carter
FISHERIES WOMAN .... Kiara Bernhardt

WHITE-WATER GUIDE ....Anna Hahn
TEACHER ....Kit Messinger
PRIEST ....Jason Min
SALMON DANCER ....Maia Luer

SYNOPSIS:

Tens of thousands of salmon died on the Lower Klamath River in 2002. The play follows a young Native woman, JULIE, as she and her family cope with the emotional, political, and economic aftermath of the fish kill and fight to save their fish and river. When JULIE meets TIM, a Klamath Basin rancher, she begins to have faith that decades of history might begin to heal if people are willing to think of a watershed as a family.

Running time is approximately two hours with one ten-minute intermission.

CHARACTERS:

(Doubling and tripling is recommended; "nn" indicates non-Native character.)

JULIE ....Will's partner; Yurok-Karuk, 20s-30s
WILL............Julie's husband, Yurok-Karuk Native fisherman, 20s-30s
ROSE..Karuk elder, Julie's grandmother, 60s
LOUISE..Julie's aunt, Yurok, 30s-40s
LITTLE MARY..............................Louise's daughter, about 8 years old
ZEEK ....Louise's son, about 10 years old
JOHNNY/CAMERAMAN .... Karuk fisherman, Will's cousin
(played by same actor as KLAMATH TRIBAL MEMBER)
ALICE (nn)...an Upper Klamath rancher, 70s
TIM (nn)...............................Alice's son, Upper Klamath rancher, 40s
BEN/GRACE (nn)..................................Tim's son (or daughter), 8–12
KATE (nn) .... Fish researcher, biology graduate student, 30s
RACHEL (nn).................................. Kate's partner, photographer, 30s
ANDY ....Chicano or Native, professor of biology

PHILLIP .... Klamath elder
WALT (nn) .... an Upper Klamath farmer, 70s
KLAMATH TRIBAL MEMBER 30s–50s
POLITICIAN (nn) .... woman, 30s–40s
REPORTER (nn) .... man or woman, 30s–40s
PRIEST (nn) .... Japanese heritage, 30s–40s
TOURISTS (nn) .... one man, one woman, 60s
(played by same actors as WALT and POLITICIAN)

Alternate characters for Town Hall, scene 12. Monologues for these characters may be found at the end of the play.

LOGGER'S DAUGHTER .... African American heritage, 20s–30s
TEACHER ...... non-Native woman married to a Klamath man, 30s–40s

SCENE BREAKDOWN:

Scene Title	**Characters in Scene**
Scene 1–Procession	Ensemble
Scene 2–Salmon Is Family	Rose, Julie, Will, Johnny, Louise, Little Mary, Zeek
Scene 3–Basin Family	Alice, Tim, Ben/Grace
Scene 4–Confluence	Rachel, Kate
Scene 5–Media Wars	Reporter
Scene 6–Telemetry	Julie, Kate, Andy
Scene 7–Tourists	Julie, Will, Tourists
Scene 8–Knowledge	Kate, Rachel, Voices
Scene 9–Lamentation	Ensemble
Scene 10–Aftermath	Kate, Rachel/Will, Andy, Julie, Johnny (parallel scenes)
Scene 11–Respects	Kate, Rachel, Louise, Rose, Julie, Little Mary, Zeek
Scene 12–Town Hall	Ensemble (internal scene: Julie,Tim)

Intermission

Scene 13–Hip-Hop	Will, Little Mary, Zeek, Ben/Grace, Reporter, Salmon Dancer
Scene 14–Tires	Rachel, Kate, Tim
Scene 15–The Visit	Julie, Tim, Will
Scene 16–Ranch Tour	Tim, Kate
Scene 17–Communion	Alice, Tim, Ben/Grace, Priest
Scene 18–Captain Jack's Stronghold	Tim
Scene 19–Ultimate Title	Alice, Tim, Ben/Grace, Phillip
Scene 20–Sacred Is	Ensemble (internal scene: Julie,Tim)

SCENIC SUGGESTIONS:

The stage should provide actors with a variety of spaces and levels. Areas for three families can be established in the early scenes and should remain consistent. Living spaces can be distinguished from outdoors with domestic props such as a rocking chair, but the illusion is largely dependent on the actors. Likewise, outdoor scenes can be suggested through sound effects (running water, birds, wind) but should be primarily an illusion maintained by the actors' relationship to space/place. Transitions should be accomplished quickly. Sometimes this may mean actors staying onstage, still and in the dark, while other scenes take place. Actors (not backstage crew) should move stools, boxes, props, and so forth as needed to set or strike each scene. Scene 12, "Town Hall," is composed primarily of monologues and can be either staged as a single scene or broken up and spliced between other scenes, functioning as transition material.

Scenic design and lighting should reflect the changes of season as follows: scenes 1–8 take place in late summer; scenes 9–11 in September; scenes 12 and 13 in the early winter months; scenes 14–17 take place in late winter; scenes 18–20 take place in springtime.

A NOTE ABOUT MULTIMEDIA USE:

During scene transitions, projections and sound effects may be used to suggest the next location, or to underscore the theme or mood of the scene. Care should be taken to avoid literal, redundant, or obvious images. Instead, photo or film images should be suggestive and evocative. The exceptions to this are underwater photography of swimming salmon; images used in scene 3, which are intended to be photos taken by Rachel of the watershed; and images we might imagine were brought to the Town Hall by citizens. The website for the Klamath Restoration Council, which keeps an archive of Klamath watershed images, is http://www.pelicannetwork.net/klamathrestoration.htm.

SOUND AND MUSIC:

We recommend that you invite people in your community to perform music or songs that belong to them. However, if recorded music or songs are used, please take care to find sources of specific Karuk, Yurok, Hupa, or Klamath/Modoc songs appropriate for use in public performance. Remember that some songs belong to individuals. Take care that you have permission to use any songs or music. Do *not* use generalized "Indian" music. Consult the tribal elders in your community for their recommendations and advice.

About props: If traditional objects, such as Brush Dance skirts or cradleboards, are borrowed from Native communities or cast members, we recommend putting the following note in the production program:

> Many of the objects used in this play belong to members of the cast or their families. They are not theatrical objects, nor are they 'artifacts.' Rather they are creations that have living spirits and are used in ceremonies and in everyday life. Baby baskets are handmade and used to keep children safe in body and spirit. The Brush Dance skirt is a living spirit, and as such a sacred ceremonial object. Please do not touch any of these objects. We are honored that the objects have come to be part of our play. *They may be handled only by the actor who uses them.*

ACT ONE

SCENE 1–PROCESSION

Late summer. Water and landscape projected. Music combined with sounds of the river, wildlife, perhaps blackbirds, osprey. SALMON DANCER enters from the back of the theatre and dances down through audience and around the stage space, then gestures to ROSE as if to say "welcome." ROSE, sitting in the audience with LITTLE MARY, rises and speaks, then walks through the audience to the stage as the other actors enter from all directions (including the audience) on their first line and move onto the stage. Projected images of salmon, water, and landscape continue throughout.

ROSE: I am Karuk.

WILL: I am Yurok.

ANDY: I am Nu-Tini-Xwe—Hupa.

JULIE: We are Yurok. We are Klamath.

WALT: I am a farmer.

ROSE: I am a basket weaver.

LITTLE MARY: I am a dancer.

WILL: We are Karuk. We are Modoc.

KATE: I am a biologist.

PRIEST: I am a priest.

ALICE: I am a rancher.

ANDY: We are Wiyot, Klamath, Yurok.

LOWER KLAMATH WOMAN: I am a social worker.

LOUISE: We are Nu-Tini-Xwe, Karuk.

REPORTER: I am a reporter.

JULIE: We are Yurok, Modoc, Karuk.

TIM: I am a rancher.

FISHERIES WOMAN: I am a fisherman's wife.

ANDY: I am a professor.

RACHEL: I am a photographer.

GUIDE: I am a business owner.

JOHNNY: I am Yurok, Karuk.

SCHOOLTEACHER: I am a teacher, a mother.

ROSE: I am an artist!

POLITICIAN: I am a politician.

WILL: I am Karuk, Tolowa.

ANDY: I am Chicano.

LOWER KLAMATH WOMAN: I am a logger's daughter.

KLAMATH MAN: I am Klamath, Modoc.

ANDY: I am at work.

WOMAN TOURIST: I am on vacation!

MAN TOURIST: Me too!

JULIE: I am at home.

ROSE: We are Wiyot, Yurok, Karuk, Nu-Tini-Xwe, Tolowa, Grand Ronde, Wasco, Warm Springs, Winnemem Wintu, Coos, Coquille, Klamath, Modoc, Siletz, Umpqua, Umatilla, Paiute, Cow Creek, Siuslaw, Takelma, Kalapuya, Shasta, Yahooskin, Chinook . . . We are!

(Movement stops; stillness for the following lines.)

ALICE: I am a mother.

WILL: I am a father.

PRIEST: I am a grandson.

ROSE: I am a grandmother. I am a daughter.

LITTLE MARY: I am a dancer!

WILL: I am Karuk, Nu-Tini-Xwe, Yurok. For my people Salmon is everything. Salmon is the center of our world, our brothers.* *(All exit dancing.)*

(Transition suggested through lighting, imagery, and/or sound.)

* In order to reflect cultural understandings, the terms River and Salmon are capitalized for Native speakers.

SCENE 2–SALMON IS FAMILY*

Late summer. The sound of laughter; actors in a pool of light go through motions of working—hauling in nets, cleaning fish, canning smoked fish; children play on the floor. The mood is joy, excitement. JULIE and WILL have an eight-month-old baby, who sleeps in a traditional cradleboard; LOUISE has two children, a boy and girl ages four and ten. Dialogue often overlaps; speaking easily and playfully as they invoke memories and tell stories for the benefit of the children.

ROSE: When we do this work we are giving thanks to the Creator for the Salmon, for the River. Salmon is the center of our world, our heart, our sustenance.

LOUISE: *(to one of her children)* Salmon is our family.

JULIE: This Anglo student in my class said to me, "How can the Salmon be your relative? You eat them?"

JOHNNY: What an idiot!

JULIE: And I told him, Salmon are our relatives because we have lived in an amazingly bonded way with them since the beginning. The connection goes much deeper than food. It's a relationship created from thousands of years of coexistence.

WILL: Tell him that all the river tribes—the Klamath, Modoc, and our people—the Yurok and Karuk—we all believe the Salmon are the spirits of our ancestors, *ĉ'iyals* come back to give life to everything.

JOHNNY: The Klamath tribes don't have the right to fish anymore!

JULIE: I don't think he'd get that.

JOHNNY: They've been cut off from the Salmon.

JULIE: He said if there are no more Salmon, just go to McDonald's!

WILL: Andy was tellin' me that they found bones of giant Salmon way up in the Upper Klamath—until then the Fish and Wildlife guys

* The stories in this scene were told by Kathleen McCovey, Heather Hostler, Nikolai Colegrove, and Lauren Taylor. Portions of WILL's lines are drawn from "Fish Kill: For the Yurok, Salmon Is Everything" by Barry McCovey Jr.

didn't even believe there were Salmon up there. They found the bones.

LOUISE: I'd tell him, Salmon is what we do in the summertime!

LITTLE MARY: My Daddy is fishing. My Daddy is on the boat, on the River.

ZEEK: When do I get my boat?

WILL: Yeah. That's how I learned, from watching my uncles, my cousins, people that are older than me. I just watched. People don't have to tell me how to do stuff step-by-step. I just watch.

JOHNNY: If you're a good listener and watch everything, you'll be good at it. I had a little boat and I was always on the River.

WILL: I became a good fisherman when I was ten years old. Because that's when you could get a fishing license and a buoy and all that, when you were ten.

ZEEK: I want a boat!

LOUISE: Not yet, next summer.

JULIE: I love the spring and summer at the mouth of the River. People from all over coming together and feeling good.

ZEEK: *(to an imaginary tourist)* Hey Mister, wanna buy a fish? My dad just caught it!

JOHNNY: What about giving it to elders and other people who can't get out to fish but love to eat it?

ZEEK: Salmon is blood on my hands and fish guts everywhere!

WILL: You take as much as you need. Always, always give fish to your elders or people who don't fish. That was always like a precious, precious thing to do is to share what you have, not just hoard it all or throw it away, you know. That is the one key thing, you know, always, always share. So every time I get a little piece, even if I don't get that much fish, I always try to give a lot of it away to others who don't get a lot of fish.

JULIE: Hey, remember me and you sleeping in a tent down by the River with the bears, sleeping by the smokehouse so the bears don't eat all the fish . . .

WILL: . . . that I worked so hard to catch. You were scared.

JULIE: You were too!

JULIE: Remember all ten of us in that small trailer, sitting around, cutting the smoked fish into pieces and stuffing them into glass jars all day long, taking bites every now and then.

(ROSE slaps her hand.)

JULIE: It was only a little!

LOUISE: Salmon was my daughter's first food. Yesterday she was saying, "When I get bigger, I can fish with my Daddy."

ROSE: In my time it was the men who caught the fish and the women who did the smoking and canning.

JULIE: Change happens, Gram.

WILL: Salmon is being part of something bigger than yourself.

ROSE: Red, full-bodied, home-seeking, home-loving, unspeaking, mysterious.

WILL: Salmon is the will to go home, the wisdom to know the way.

JULIE: Remember home, the smell of home, the smell of that current, that particular place, that turn up the estuary, into the downward current, that cool scent of feeder creeks.

WILL: Salmon is headstrong!

JOHNNY: Salmon knows lots of things I don't know.

ZEEK: That's for sure!

(Transition suggested through lighting, imagery, and/or sound.)

SCENE 3—BASIN FAMILY*

Late summer. In another area of the stage, ALICE stands looking out over her land. Then, as if time has passed, she sits in the rocker.

---

* ALICE's opening monologue is adapted from "Yainix Journal" by Becky Hatfield Hyde; details have been fictionalized.

ALICE: We woke that morning to three feet of snow around the house, and the roads drifting shut within minutes of plowing track. My husband worried about feeding the hungry calves. Timmy spun circles in the deep snow, spinning and spinning in bright red boots until his blue coat spun off in the wind. . . . When I married, I married this land. In my mind it was all about coming to this ranch, the natural beauty, and fixing the River. Fixing everything. Paint the old dingy house. Fence the River. Dig thistles. Clean the shop. Chainsaw down the old fence, build some new fence. The hardest realization for me this season is that what's really changing is me . . .

(A conversation they have had in some form before about an ongoing and painful issue)

ALICE: *(sits in a rocker)* Did you talk to him?

TIM: I did.

ALICE: Call him back. I'll talk to him. You can't sue your own family!

TIM: No you won't. And yes you can. You're the one always saying this family is a business. Well Greg's married into Walt's family and that sure as hell is a business—about seven thousand acres of business. They need the allocation. It's a drought comin' on and without it they're belly up.

ALICE: Get me the phone.

TIM: The hearing is scheduled for next week. Water board'll decide. Lawyers'll decide, just like they always do. Is there more o' that cobbler?

ALICE: You raise 'em up straight, give 'em the fear of God, and healthy respect for Nature, and love of the land, and they turn around and sue your water rights out from under you.

TIM: (*under his breath*) Sorta like what we did to the Indians.

ALICE: I heard that and no it's not, that's different. It's that Mac Hardy. I knew he's a greedy son-of-a-bitch when your father and he played poker on Wednesdays. Always drunk our beer and never brought any. I was pregnant with you then. I couldn't sleep and I'd watch them from the landing upstairs, and that Hardy he'd get a look in his eye outa some old western movie.

TIM: *(He has heard all this before.)* It's not personal, Mom. Isn't that what you always tell Phillip?

ALICE: That's different.

TIM: How? Indians should not get the share of the water they need but they should not take it personally? But we can? Tell that to Captain Jack! The land Greg and Walt farm was massive wetlands that the government drained . . .

ALICE: This is family!

TIM: I hardly know what family means anymore. Seems to me not having fish to feed your family is pretty damn personal. I'm going up. I got paperwork. Need anything?

ALICE: Is Ben [Grace] asleep?

TIM: Yeah. Out like a light. Good night. Use the buzzer like they showed you when you're ready.

ALICE: Help me to the porch, would you son? *(He does so.)* Look there, the Milky Way is so clear it's reflected in the marsh.

(Transition suggested through lighting, imagery, and/or sound.)

SCENE 4—CONFLUENCE

RACHEL is viewing her most recent photographs on her laptop. As she forwards from slide to slide, the images are projected on the rear scrim, or in some other place the audience can see. The images take us on a visual tour of the Klamath River below Iron Gate Dam. RACHEL and KATE are used to finishing one another's sentences.

KATE: Wow, now that's a great shot!

RACHEL: Iron Gate Dam.

KATE: You can totally see the algae growing in the reservoir. Makes you wonder what they were thinking in 1909.

RACHEL: Electricity, Baby!

KATE: Irrigation. *(pause; more slides)* That's Ishi Pishi Falls!

RACHEL: The birthplace of the Karuk people.

(KATE snorts; RACHEL gives her a look.)

KATE: I'm sorry. I'm agnostic, what can I say? Christians believe they came from some garden called Eden; and the Karuk believe . . . my mind just doesn't work that way!

RACHEL: What way is that?

KATE: Mythically . . . or . . .

RACHEL: That's because you've decided that something can either be a fiction or a fact. There are whole ways of knowing that have nothing to do with your sexy quantitative mind.

KATE: Are you diss-ing me, girlfriend?

RACHEL: You were being irreverent.

KATE: I'll show you irreverent! *(tackles and tickles her while her computer continues to change slides every 5–8 seconds)*

RACHEL: Hey! . . . you . . . stop it . . . okay, okay!

(Both women are laughing, breathless.)

KATE: Oh my God, it's doing it on its own! *(more laughter)*

RACHEL: That's the Salmon River . . . *(She hits "pause.")*

KATE: I'll miss you. I wish you'd just come with us.

RACHEL: I just got home.

KATE: You just don't like science types.

RACHEL: That's not true. There was a wildlife girl in the photo workshop last month.

KATE: Oh really? And you wouldn't go on the river with me, but . . .

RACHEL: I just didn't know you'd be going out there. If you'd told me your schedule sooner, we could have planned the trip together. You count fish, I shoot pictures, but you can't seem to let me know what you're doing one minute to the next. (new slide) What? Are you afraid of being out to your colleagues?

KATE: Uh, no-oh. They're cool.

RACHEL: Fine.

KATE: I'm sorry. Next time, I promise, 'kay? *(RACHEL is silent, forwards slides.)* Hey, that's Weitchpec, where the Trinity and the Klamath meet . . . do you know why the Trinity water is so much clearer than the Klamath?

RACHEL: No-oh. *(She's heard this before.)*

KATE: Well . . . because it doesn't carry the same kind of silt load. It's colder. Most of Trinity River is dammed up at Shasta and sent down to central California for big ag; but on this side of the Shasta dam the Trinity runs through protected wilderness. We should go camping there. The Klamath on the other hand has to be everything to everybody. You have farmers and ranchers in Oregon using the headwaters—all the cattle crap, and the pesticides. Then through seven or so dams. Then logging and mining along the midriver—more silt. What you see there, at the confluence, is the result of the river's long, toxic journey: the clear, cold Trinity running into the warmer, greener, dirtier Klamath.

RACHEL: *(as if she is tasting the word)* Confluence. It's a beautiful word, isn't it? Say it.

BOTH WOMEN: Confluence . . . *(They tumble into an embrace and kiss.)*

(Transition suggested through lighting, imagery, and/or sound.)

SCENE 5–MEDIA WARS

REPORTER is on location with CAMERAMAN, getting ready to go on camera; checks hair, perhaps rubs out a cigarette.

REPORTER: Okay, you ready? Yeah, good to go.

CAMERAMAN: On my mark. *(holds up fingers as he counts)* We're hot in five, four, three, two . . . *(He signals her.)*

REPORTER: Good evening. I'm standing on the border of Oregon and California in some of the most beautiful country I've ever seen, but that beauty disguises a troubled landscape. The Klamath River

Basin has become a prime example of a problem facing the entire West: how to share limited water with farmers guaranteed irrigation rights by the federal government, fish protected by the Endangered Species Act, and Indian tribes with treaties promising their fisheries will go on forever. In the early twentieth century, before the United States government drained Tule Lake and began "reclamation" of the land, this whole area was underwater, and the natural fishing grounds of the Klamath and Modoc people. The Klamath were salmon people too—some elders have claimed that salmon existed even in the Upper Klamath. Recently, tribal anthropologists found bones of a huge salmon. But salmon were not the only "big fish" in these waters. The suckerfish—or Cwaam [chwaam] as the Klamath call it—is a sacred resource to tribal communities. It can grow to four feet long. Historical records indicate that the Klamath fishermen brought in ten thousand pounds of suckerfish in one season. Now, like the salmon before it, this once plentiful fish has dwindled. Suckerfish are, like the coho salmon, protected under the Endangered Species Act. Last year farmers in the Klamath River Basin saw their crops shrivel as the federal government cut irrigation water to protect the suckerfish. Downriver, the Hupa, Yurok, and Karuk tribes consider the salmon a critical part of their livelihood as well as spiritual life, and now this fish, which used to be so plentiful that tribal elders claim "you could walk across the river on the backs of salmon," is threatened too. This year the Yurok Tribe of northern California has warned the federal government that a fish kill of unprecedented magnitude could devastate the salmon runs. President Bush has repeatedly pledged to do all he can for the farmers, but full irrigation means less water for the suckerfish and the salmon.

REPORTER: *(off-camera now, to CAMERAMAN, who is Karuk)* Hey, was there really a time when you could walk across the river on the backs of salmon?

CAMERAMAN: Heck yeah—just talk to my Gram!

(Transition suggested through lighting, imagery, and/or sound.)

SCENE 6–TELEMETRY*

River sounds. JULIE and KATE, both students of ANDY, are working over imaginary holding pens, putting tracking devices in the fish, then letting them go into the river. The action—holding up the little temperature recorder; capturing and holding a live, struggling salmon; measuring it, and then releasing—should be specifically researched and then mimed throughout the scene until JULIE and KATE's conversation escalates.

ANDY: *(explaining to JULIE; KATE has done this before and demonstrates)* Salmon are what's called a keystone species. They benefit all the other species of plants and animals of the watershed by bringing ocean nutrients all the way upriver, making the trees grow twice as fast.

JULIE: Yeah, that's what my Gram always says.

ANDY: We put a tracker in the esophagus of the fish. We try to track ten fish a week.

KATE: Last summer we did about a hundred fish.

ANDY: There is a temperature recorder glued to each transmitter. We can download information off the temperature recorder.

KATE: Okay, watch close. (*demonstrating*) Pick 'em up real gentle like this, see? They've already had enough trauma. Easy there, this is gonna help us help you, Brother Salmon.

ANDY: The data from the temperature recorder will help us prove that when the river is too warm fish are more prone to disease—and that's why we're worried about a fish kill.

KATE: If we can prove that the fish are trying to get out of the warm-ass river into the cold creeks . . .

JULIE: *(measuring the fish KATE is holding)* Here's what I don't get. Indians lived their lives understanding the tides and the river. We knew how to survive for thousands of years on this river. Isn't that

* Portions of this scene were drawn from the research and reflective writing of Heather Hostler.

proof enough that we know what we are talking about? Tribal biologists have already warned of a fish kill this year.

ANDY: Yeah, but the federal government wants data. The Indians' data was a different kind of data—it was an oral society, knowledge handed down through generations. Now we have to go back and quantify that body of knowledge.

JULIE: It was a way of life. My Gram says we should be doing the First Salmon Ceremony—like they did a hundred years ago.

ANDY: Are there folks who know the First Salmon Ceremony anymore?

JULIE: She says we should be doing it. She says it's our part . . .

ANDY: I like to think about it this way—Indian people have always made good use of the tools the Creator has given. Science is a tool. If people can use it to help the salmon, that's a good thing. *(They tag, measure, and release another fish.)* So, are we good to go here? I'm going to check on the other teams. *(exits)*

(JULIE and KATE both continue the movement of tagging, measuring, and releasing the fish.)

JULIE: I saw you on TV.

KATE: Oh God, I so sucked. I felt like I let everyone down. The reporter just made me seem like some rabid environmentalist. Rachel says it's the dreads.

JULIE: It's not your hair. It's anti-Indian rhetoric. It's all the pro-farmer propaganda. Same ol' same ol' stuff.

KATE: I could have not fallen over myself. *(changing the subject)* Did Andy tell you about the stakeholders meeting next month?

JULIE: Yeah.

KATE: Are you going?

JULIE: No.

KATE: You should go. The last one didn't have a single tribal person there.

JULIE: Figures.

KATE: The tribes should be part of this conversation. What?

JULIE: I'm sorry, I just wish you wouldn't tell me what I need, or what I should do. You don't have the kind of stake in this issue that Native people do and you shouldn't be telling us what to do.

KATE: Excuse me, I care about the river and the fish. It's what I've chosen to do with my life.

JULIE: It's different for my people. For us, Salmon is everything—subsistence, culture, history, identity. It's who we are!

KATE: Ordinary citizens can't have the same investment in caring for the planet?

JULIE: All I'm saying is that for you it's about being right; it's about winning; about "saving the environment" as if that's something other than yourself. For us it's about being whole, staying alive.

KATE: It's about being alive for all of us. Everything we do in our culture has an impact, every choice, what we drive, what we buy or buy into.

JULIE: But for us the threat of extermination is immediate, just like it is for the fish. You come here doing your research that will eventually get you some good agency job. You care, sure, but if the Salmon go extinct, you'll find some other species to save. For my family, if the Salmon don't survive my grandmother will die of a broken spirit. You called that fish "Brother" . . .

KATE: When?

JULIE: A couple minutes ago—but it's a metaphor for you. It's not a metaphor for us! My people have lived here for ten thousand years or more. *(increasingly angry as if something unstoppable is welling up from within her)* My people live here. They die here! They are the trees, the water, the fish. That the Salmon are brothers is not some kind of myth; the Salmon are not symbols of life, they are life. We have maintained a healthy balance with the River and the Salmon and everything else because it's all one body, one family. If the Salmon die, we break apart; the Salmon make life make sense!

(pause)

KATE: When are you going to say that to the people who need to hear it? *(She picks up equipment and moves away.)*

(ANDY, who has overheard some of the conversation, reenters the scene.)

ANDY: Hey.

JULIE: She just pisses me off sometimes. I don't know what it is. I get sick of her trying to "advocate" for us, telling me how to protect what's already mine! Our people's! The water rights belong to us and were promised to us by treaty long before greedy white potato farmers dammed up our river and killed our fish with pesticides.

ANDY: You ought to go to that stakeholders meeting. *(SALMON DANCER may appear here.)*

JULIE: I haven't got the money, and Will is already pissed off I'm doing this. And I don't have a babysitter.

ANDY: I can get you school funds. Take your baby with you—lots of people bring their kids.

JULIE: I'll think about it.

(Transition suggested through lighting, imagery, and/or sound.)

SCENE 7–TOURISTS*

JULIE and WILL at home. He gathers some gear and heads out the door. JULIE follows him, the baby on a cradleboard in her arms.

JULIE: Where are you going? Can you give me some money first? I need ten dollars. I need to buy food and stuff for her. (*WILL exits.*) Don't slam the door! Where are you going? (*Pause. She turns and speaks to the audience.*) My mother was born to a full-blooded Yurok woman, raised on the Klamath River. My ancestors go all the way back to the beginning of time. My great-great-great grandfather was named Peck-Wan John. This means that I have ancestors who lived at Pecwan, upriver. My great-grandmother was born in Klamath in 1909. She lived just upriver from Requa, by where the Golden Bears Bridge

* This scene was developed from reflective writings by Lauren Taylor.

is now. Now I'm involved in this terribly intense relationship . . . the father of my child . . . he's a subsistence fisherman, Yurok-Karuk. He grew up downriver, but now he fishes like an upriver guy, with a dip net. He says he gets closer to the fish, closer to the River that way.

(During the following, WILL, with a long dip net, JOHNNY [his "clubber"], and one of the children are silhouetted high on a rock or fishing platform at the back of the stage.)

JULIE: I gave a farmer from Bakersfield a ride the other day—this tourist and his wife with her humongous white purse. They'd locked their keys in their big white truck. *(MAN and WOMAN TOURIST enter the scene and become part of JULIE's story, sitting in the backseat of her car.)* So I gave them a ride to their big white camper to get the spare key. They were bragging about how many fish they were taking home to wherever. They had a huge cooler in the back of their huge white truck. In the car with them, I'm suddenly aware that I smell like fish guts because I'd been chopping heads off all morning, getting it ready for smoking.

MAN TOURIST: Water seems low this year.

JULIE: I can see his wife in my rearview in the backseat, scowling. Might as well dive in, I think; after all, how many times do you get to be face-to-face with one of them? *(to the TOURIST)* Farmers upriver in the Klamath Basin turned the water off. You're probably using some of our water, aren't you?

MAN: I'm from Bakersfield myself. Been a farmer all my life. That's why I moved to Bakersfield.

JULIE: Isn't that part of the Sacramento Valley? Did you know seventy percent of the Trinity River, which flows into the Klamath, is diverted down south to farms like yours?

MAN TOURIST: No, we're not using your water. We have a private pump. And we have aqueducts. Our water comes from the San Joaquin and the Kern. . . . So, uh, are you going to school?

JULIE: Yeah, Native American studies major, with a focus on environmental law. Our tribe needs good lawyers to protect our water rights.

MAN TOURIST: We're having dinner at Steelhead tonight, with some friends of ours. It's our thirtieth wedding anniversary. We've made it that long.

JULIE: Hey, Happy Anniversary! I've eaten there once. I had the lobster.

WOMAN: We love lobster! We had real Maine lobster *in Maine.* We've had fresh Alaska salmon on an *Alaskan cruise.* We've had this wonderful Cajun crawdad stew, in New Orleans. We even had buffalo steak in Wyoming!

MAN: Yep, we put twenty-four thousand miles on our camper touring the country. Sometimes I feel like I'm retracing my own ancestors' migration West! When we retired we sold our house and now we can go wherever we want and see all the things we've missed. We've earned it! This is what we worked for all our lives. That's what our friends say.

(TOURISTS dissolve into the shadows, leaving JULIE alone.)

JULIE: When I dropped him off, he tried to give me twenty dollars. No thanks, really, I don't need anything. But he insisted *(pulls a $20 bill out of pocket)*, so I took it. For the fish. For our daughter.

(Transition suggested through lighting, imagery, and/or sound.)

SCENE 8–KNOWLEDGE*

KATE downstage looking into the river. She's been working but stops as if mesmerized by the fish. Meanwhile, RACHEL, upstage, has been shooting pictures. VOICES speak from shadows. Moving images of salmon may be projected. SALMON DANCER appears and disappears.

MALE VOICE (WILL): The Creator cried and the Salmon were born. The Salmon gave themselves to the Human People.

---

* Portions of this scene were adapted from the reflective writings of Heather Hostler and Jessica Eden.

KATE: One theory says that Salmon navigate by the stars. Feeling the stars in their bones.

FEMALE VOICE (ROSE): Salmon smell the high country. It's in their blood. There is memory in the blood.

KATE: (*to the Salmon*) Do you call out to one another? Do you sing with joy when you smell it, when you make that turn from the big River up your own fond creek? Do you echo one another in some unknown language, some dark memory place your ancestors knew?

MALE VOICE (WILL): The same spirit goes up and down the River, the fish changes, but the spirit remains.

KATE: How do they know when it's time?

FEMALE VOICE (LOUISE or JULIE): How do you know when you are hungry?

KATE: Sometimes it hits me when I'm out here checking the equipment, trying to gather information to protect them: they are knowledge, they embody it.

MALE VOICE (WILL): Salmon is all time . . .

FEMALE VOICE (ROSE): Ancient time, old one . . .

FEMALE VOICE (LOUISE or JULIE): Keeper of knowledge . . .

MALE VOICE (WILL): Keeper of time.

(SALMON DANCER or company may create a transition here through movement; or the transition may be lighting and sound only.)

SCENE 9—LAMENTATION*

LOUISE: It was just after one of the Jump Dances in the fall. We were all exhausted and ready for a feast. The women were getting ready at the long tables and the men were hanging up the regalia. Kids were running around and we were all happy and laughing. My

* LOUISE's opening monologue was inspired by community comments following the first public reading of the play-in-progress. We regret not noting the name of the woman who told this story.

grandson, who was four, was always talking about how he couldn't wait to fish with his daddy and his grampa, but the men wouldn't let him out there. "When you're bigger than the fish," my father would say, "that's when you can catch one!" So that day, we're laughing and talking and happy. Where's my son? Down by the water across the path there where the grass breaks and the sand begins. He's okay. *(ZEEK enters, proud, barely able to hold a huge representative salmon.)* Then I hear his voice and we all turn around and there he is with a great big Salmon draped across his two little arms. Straining and fighting to keep standing, he's so happy, crying out . . .

ZEEK: Look, Mama, I caught a fish! I caught it myself! I caught a fish!

LOUISE: *(taking it)* That fish was dead; it was already dead.

(Pause, as the rhythmic beat begins.)

REPORTER lines and the lamentation must seem simultaneous. The actors and director should work to make sure that the words of both are understood, even though voices may overlap. Under the lamentation, a drum, or the men's rhythmic song from the Brush Dance. As the lamentation and news report are spoken, the representational fish brought onstage by ZEEK is passed in a slow and respectful manner from person to person. The intensity and volume of the lamentation increase gradually until the REPORTER is nearly drowned out.

JULIE: Thirty thousand and counting.

ALL: As they return.

LOUISE: Forty thousand salmon dead.

ALL: As they return.

JOHNNY: Fifty thousand and counting.

ALL: As they return.

("As they return" whispered under the REPORTER's lines.)

REPORTER: Chinook salmon, coho salmon, and steelhead continue to litter the shores of the Klamath River in one of the worst fish kills in US history. Tribal spokespersons say the die-off was a direct consequence of the refusal by the US Bureau of Reclamation to release more water into the river. The reduced flow on the Klamath River resulted in higher than normal water temperatures—conditions that foster disease in salmon. Adult salmon returning upriver to spawn and juveniles migrating downriver are hurt or killed by high water temperatures and poor water quality due to reduced flows. Temperatures above sixty degrees can be fatal to salmon, and temperatures in the Klamath River in the weeks prior to the kill were well into the high seventies.

WILL: Gill rot!

ALL: As they return. (*This line repeats as a whisper under the REPORTER's lines.*)

REPORTER: Last year, farmers stormed the headgates of A-Canal—one of the irrigation channels that takes water out of Tule Lake—demanding more water for potato, alfalfa, and hay. The farmers' protest was an illegal act in direct violation of the EPA ruling. Nevertheless, Secretary of Interior Gale Norton pledged ample water this year. Meanwhile, tribal and commercial fishermen and environmental groups recently filed litigation challenging the federal government's allocation of water to the agricultural Klamath Basin during a drought year.

(REPORTER pauses, letting the lamentation stand alone until next REPORTER line below.)

ANDY: Thirty thousand and counting.

ALL: As they return.

LOUISE: Forty thousand salmon dead.

ALL: As they return.

JOHNNY: Sixty thousand salmon dead.

ALL: As they return.

WILL: Gill rot!

ALL: As they return.

ROSE: Seventy thousand dead.

ALL: As they return.

(*ALL are quiet, still, as the REPORTER continues.*)

REPORTER: The question now is: What will they do with the bodies? Dead fish lie decomposing along thirty miles of the river. Last weekend a handful of volunteers gathered some of the debris. It was later composted with sawdust and woodchips.

(*The rhythmic lamentation resumes, growing in intensity; men keep the beat; perhaps a drum.*)

ROSE: The fishermen abandoned their nets.

ALL: As they return.

WILL: We counted them. We hacked their tails off.

ALL: As they return.

JULIE: Leaving the bodies open, bellies to the sun.

ALL: As they return.

ROSE: Floating—each its own shipwreck of life.

ALL: As they return.

JULIE: Each not only a meal but a life.

ALL: As they return.

JULIE: Seventy thousand dead in heaving waves of flesh.

ALL: As they return.

ROSE: As if these sweet ones are litter, not corpses of our underwater families.

ALL: As they return.

ANDY: Those who would have, in any other year, in any other time, been setting nets in the sun, teaching our children . . .

WILL: Mostly I left them there. I wanted people to see them, to smell them.

ALL: As they return.

ROSE: Who picked up these dead and dying ones?

ALL: As they return.

ROSE: Who laid them to rest, mixed their flesh with woodchips and ash?

ALL: As they return.

ROSE: Carried them one at a time, for some were three feet long.

ALL: As they return.

ROSE: Who witnessed, who was not driven back by the smell?

ALL: As they return.

JULIE: We carried them in our arms, on our backs, in our hearts.

WILL: We counted them.

ALL: As they return.

ROSE: We carry them still. In our arms, on our backs, in our hearts.

(*Transition suggested through lighting, imagery, and/or sound.*)

SCENE 10–AFTERMATH*

Same location as scene 3.

RACHEL: How's Julie?

KATE: Crazy with grief, what do you expect? For her family it's a holocaust, ya know?

RACHEL: Yeah, actually I do.

KATE: I didn't mean it that way.

RACHEL: I know . . . We should go visit her family.

KATE: (*hardly hearing*) You work and you work and you count the juveniles, open the creeks, you move the sites, you fight with the white-water guides and the miners and the dope dealers, you try to talk to the feds and the farmers, you interpret the data and then you get more

* RACHEL's dialogue was drawn from the words of Nicole Barchilon Frank and the writings of Rabbi Zalman Schachter-Shalomi. For more about National Marine Fisheries Service biologist Michael Kelly, see "Salmon Experts Pressured to Change Findings," Union of Concerned Scientists, accessed July 25, 2013, http://www.ucsusa.org/scientific_integrity/abuses_of_science/klamath-river-salmon.html.

data, you write opinions and then get pressure from the feds to change the data, but all in all you think things are getting better. You think, well at least in this river we haven't started putting them on trucks and driving them upriver! And then this . . . this . . . death. We predicted it. We did predict it! Hurrah for science! Andy has already had to tell some families that they've caught their quota; now he has to explain to them why there are suddenly fifty thousand dead salmon on the riverbank?! It's only my damn dissertation, but for the tribes, Salmon is everything. What am I doing, Rach? How did I ever think that I could make a damn difference?

(*pause*)

RACHEL: (*comforting her physically in some way*) In Hebrew the word for "universe" also means "fabric," "garment." And the fabric is being torn everywhere. When we do mitzvahs—good actions—it's like we're reaching up and helping to mend the torn fabric of the universe.

KATE: It's not a tear, it's a huge rip, it's a gash.

(cross fade to WILL and others below)

WILL: We told them! Before the fish kill happened, we told them there was going to be a fish kill. We said you're gonna devastate our fishery if water levels go any lower. We've got written documents that showed them . . .

ANDY: I wrote some of those reports! The Yurok Tribe predicted this; Department of Fish and Game—California and Federal—predicted it; the Karuk Tribe predicted it.

WILL: Hell, my grandmother predicted it!

JOHNNY: Yeah, but she don't talk cash, man.

ANDY: They don't even listen to their own US biologists! They knew there would be a disaster if the levels were too low.

WILL: That guy Michael Kelly at National Marine Fisheries wrote two scientific reports advocating for higher river flows in order to save coho salmon. His reports were squashed . . .

JULIE: Quashed . . .

WILL: Quashed, whatever.

ANDY: Low water levels cause high water temperatures, and that causes disease that kills.

JULIE: The Department of Interior forced biologists to alter their reports in favor of less water. How can they justify giving more water to farmers when this is a drought year for everyone?

JOHNNY: 'Cause farmers give big bucks to the Bush campaign, that's why!

WILL: Salmon are not going to survive.

JOHNNY: Buffalo didn't.

(*Transition suggested through lighting, imagery, and/or sound.*)

SCENE 11–RESPECTS*

Same location as scene 2. KATE and RACHEL visit JULIE's family. Only the women and children are there. Only necessary props such as rugelach, jars, basket, Brush Dance skirt, dip net should be used to suggest activities. Feeling awkward and out of place, KATE sits on the floor interacting with the children; RACHEL sits near ROSE. The stroller may also be present.

ZEEK: Can I have another one?

LOUISE: One.

ZEEK: What's the name of them again?

RACHEL: Rugelach.

ZEEK: Is that an old name?

LOUISE: He means is it Yurok. He calls it the old language.

RACHEL: It's Yiddish. Which is old, but not as old as Yurok.

LOUISE: Go on, take another one for Little Mary too, and then go outside.

---

* Portions of this scene were drawn from the stories and reflective writings of Kathleen McCovey, Lauren Taylor, Nikolai Colegrove, and Heather Hostler.

ZEEK: My uncle and grandpa are out getting dead fish. I found the first one. There's tons of them!

LITTLE MARY: They stink!

ZEEK: We saw them from the bus. They had to cut the tails off.

LOUISE: Go on now.

LITTLE MARY: My teacher was crying. They sent us home from school. My dad was crying.

LOUISE: That's enough. Both of you go out and play.

(*The children take more rugelach and leave; an awkward pause.*)

ROSE: It's nice of you to come see us.

LOUISE: Yes, thank you for the sweets—sugar's always good medicine!

RACHEL: Thank you. This is a terrible thing that has happened to you.

KATE: We're so so sorry.

(*Awkward pause; ROSE is working willow root for basket weaving.*)

RACHEL: What are you making?

ROSE: This is the willow root. Willow roots to make your baskets and the caps like this one we wear in the dances. When I go down to the River and pick the willow roots, I'm on my hands and knees. My hands and fingers are in that dirt pulling on that long twine to pull the root out, and then going home, soaking it and peeling it—like Louise is doing. You know that's a whole process with the earth.

RACHEL: Then when you wear the cap your thoughts are deep like the roots and flowing like the River.

ROSE: You got it! (*laughs*) I like this girl, Kate, she knows.

RACHEL: How do you get the colors?

ROSE: To make the red, I use the bark of the red alder tree. The black color comes from the stems of the five-finger fern and the white color comes from beargrass. When I want to make a really fancy basket, I put yellow in it. I dye porcupine quills yellow with that mountain moss, you know, that one that grows high up in the trees in the high country.

KATE: *Letharia vulpina*—wolf lichen.

ROSE: We just call it moss. You see, to the Karuk people everything and everyone has a purpose. The spirit people taught the Karuk how to live on the land, what to do, what to eat, how to behave, and how and when to conduct ceremonies. Then when the Karuk people knew what to do, the spirit people went into the sky, the earth, the trees, the animals, the rocks, and into the plants. You see, when I am in the forest, I am never alone, I am surrounded by spirit people.

JULIE: Try telling that to a forester!

ROSE: I have!

(*In the way that some things seem hilarious at a funeral, the moment provokes peals of laughter, which breaks what is left of the ice.*)

KATE: How is Will doing?

JULIE: When I saw his face when he came home the first day when he saw the fish dead, I thought someone in our family had died. He was too upset to express any emotion. He got up at three a.m. one night and just started writing his heart out. He's never done that before.

LOUISE: It seems as if we are struggling to hold on.

JULIE: It just hit us so hard. We feed salmon to our babies before they can talk or walk. It's like it's our blood spilled.

ROSE: It is a big hurt and cry for all our people. Our life on the River lay rotting. What do we do? We have to get down and pray.

LOUISE: It was like how it feels when you grieve for a family member that has passed on—that heavy feeling in your gut. I cut my hair off to honor the death of my relative, the Salmon.

ROSE: That's what we women do when someone dies.

LOUISE: When you have a funeral there's an event; there's a grieving time. Elders have never heard about anything like this fish kill in our legends or stories.

(*pause*)

ROSE: (*finding courage for all of them*) Salmon have seen death all around them, but they still fight back. They are strong! Watching them always makes my heart glad.

JULIE: It keeps coming to me that through our medicine we should be able to do something about the fish kill. Why can't we fix this?

LOUISE: Did we do something that caused this to happen?

(*In the following, ROSE's lines can be a monologue, a unified train of thought, almost an invocation to prayer.*)

ROSE: My mind takes me to a time when we thrived as healthy people. A time when only our people managed this beautiful land.

LOUISE: How can a system that has been perfected over thousands of years be discarded so easily? Not even two hundred years later a catastrophe has devastated that abundance.

JULIE: Because upriver they drained the lakes and built the dams to use the water for irrigation "to feed America" after the war.

LOUISE: Hey, don't go there right now. You know Gram doesn't like politics.

ROSE: During this time there would be the First Salmon Ceremony and a feast that gave thanks to the Salmon for giving their lives for the survival of the people. This was something that has never been done in my lifetime.*

JULIE: Why don't we try to bring the First Salmon Ceremony back and use it as healing?

ROSE: All the men had a meeting down at Requa and they were standing around talking about what they should do. And out there in the water there was a sea lion splashing and throwing Salmon around. That was a prayer time. That was a prayer time.

LOUISE: I guess some of us feel a sense of shame, a sense of responsibility.

---

* In 1994 Agnes Baker Pilgrim of the Takelma Tribe began performing the Sacred Salmon Ceremony on the Rogue River in Oregon, where it had not been done for about 150 years. While the Klamath and the Rogue are different watersheds, both rivers are salmon spawning rivers and sustained indigenous cultures that had their own annual salmon ceremonies.

ROSE: There is a difference between blame and responsibility. We have a relationship that needs tending. When I was a child the River gave me a prayer and I sewed it into my Brush Dance skirt.* Let me show you something. (*starts to rise*)

JULIE: I'll get it, Gram.

ROSE: Get me my Brush Dance skirt. In that suitcase there. No, not that one. The blue one there. That one. Bring me that here. (*JULIE brings out a shelled Brush Dance skirt and ROSE takes it; the sound of the ocean rises from the skirt.*) This skirt Little Mary will wear.

RACHEL/KATE: (*Kate moves around to see better.*) It's beautiful!

(*Julie unpacks the other skirt; JULIE and either ROSE or LOUISE hold the skirt up and walk with it.*)

ROSE: I made this. My grandfather and I took this deer when he was about eighty and he could not see anymore. After my grandfather passed away, I took these two hides out of the freezer and had them tanned. I then made a skirt from them, to honor my grandfather. I picked up almost all of these abalone and olivella shells myself. This skirt took a few years to make. Almost everything in this dress comes from nature and from my memories.

RACHEL: Feel how heavy it is.

KATE: Wow!

ROSE: Listen. Can you hear it?

RACHEL/KATE: It sounds exactly like the ocean!

ROSE: (*LITTLE MARY comes back, drawn by the skirt and the stories.*) This is the skirt you will wear, Little Mary!

LOUISE: I am so glad my daughter gets to dance! I remember my first summer camp was at Requa by the Brush Dance pit. I was a counselor. When she was two and a half she was absolutely entranced by the dancers in the pit. She began slowly bobbing up and down the way

* The Brush Dance is a ceremony to heal a sick child or other community member. The Jump Dance, mentioned in the play and by Kathleen McCovey in her essay in this volume, is for the purpose of world peace and community healing.

the girls are supposed to. My heart filled with joy. You will dance! It's coming up soon.

LITTLE MARY: Did you finish my cap?!

LOUISE: Almost!

JULIE: Me and my cousin would always be so tired after a long night of Brush Dancing, and we would always play this little game where one of us would stay awake and watch the other fall asleep only to be scared awake again by one of us shaking the other.

ROSE: You don't have to be a tribal member to go. We have the dances out at Patrick's Point you can go to, or come up to Orleans when we have ours.

RACHEL: Thank you, we'd love to. (*pause*)

ROSE: My grandpa used to tell me a story about a rock out by the Orick beach: a lady used to live out there on that rock eating clams, oysters, and mussels. When I was little I had always believed it. I made up my mind that if I ever had the chance to go and see if it were true or not, I wouldn't go. I have believed in the lady who lived off the sea ever since.

(*ZEEK has come back, drawn by his great-Gram's stories.*)

LITTLE MARY: (*to RACHEL*) Have you ever gone eeling?

RACHEL: What's eeling?

LITTLE MARY: Catching eels. Some people think only boys can do it, but I really want to.

ZEEK: They don't catch 'em, they hook 'em! They have this long stick, like an arm, with a hook. They just dip it in and get an eel.

LITTLE MARY: I saw a pretty one that was all carved on the handle.

RACHEL: I hope you get to do it someday.

JULIE: You will.

KATE: We should probably get going. I'm supposed to be out there helping Will.

JULIE: Thank you for coming.

LOUISE: Thank you for the rugelach.

(*ROSE gives them a jar of smoked salmon.*)

ROSE: *My* gram's recipe!

RACHEL: Thank you, Rose.

KATE: Bye, take care.

(*They exit.*)

ROSE: Nice girls.

JULIE: They're lesbians, Gram.

ROSE: I know. You think I was born yesterday? (*JULIE laughs.*)

(*Transition suggested through lighting, imagery, and/or sound.*)

SCENE 12–TOWN HALL*

Staging options: the Town Hall is a series of monologues that can be presented as a single scene, in which case actors should take care to listen, respond, and engage with one another to build believable tension over the issues discussed. Alternatively, these monologues can be arranged as interludes by placing them between other scenes, in which case the Town Hall serves as an overarching metaphor for the entire production. In either case, individual monologues can be reordered, swapped out (see alternate monologues at end of play), or cut down depending on production needs.

A month or so later; early winter. The location overlooks the mouth of the Klamath River, a few miles from the Yurok Tribal Headquarters where the imaginary Town Hall meeting is to take place.

REPORTER: (*on camera, interviewing ROSE*) I'm standing high above the mouth of the Klamath River looking down on the site of the 2002

* Portions of the REPORTER and WHITE-WATER GUIDE's lines are drawn from the research and writing of Holly Couling. Portions of the community voices of the Town Hall were inspired by participants in the stakeholder meetings facilitated by Consensus Associates' Bob Chadwick and Terry Morton and have been fictionalized to preserve privacy.

fish kill. This is where Yurok and Karuk tribal fishermen make their livings, and this is where they are losing that living. The situation really hits home for one tribal elder, who grew up on smoked salmon and acorn soup.

ROSE: I wonder how many generations of people these rocks have seen. They never get tired of watching their friend the ocean roll in and out. I bet that these rocks and ocean are good old friends and take in all that they see. These rocks are the first to see the Salmon returning. These two old friends, the rocks and ocean, must have wept and grieved when they saw the Salmon floating on their sides, gills rotting, devastated spirits. You'd see dead fish from time to time but I've never seen what's going on now. It's real hard to take, seeing them die like that.

(*As REPORTER speaks, citizens enter and sit in a loose circle; some may stand, pace, change position; children on the floor may have busywork, coloring books, perhaps; the elder women may have handwork.*)

REPORTER: (*on camera*) Salmon are amazing. Born knowing this river and their place in it. Traveling the same way their ancestors have done for centuries. Now, here at the mouth of the Klamath River, the salmon themselves have called a Town Hall meeting. Farmers and ranchers from the Upper Klamath Basin, midriver folks, and Lower Klamath tribal fisheries experts and community members have come together in a series of stakeholder meetings to discuss what must be seen as a shared future. How do you balance the water level of a river when agriculturalists and commercial fishermen depend on it for money, consumers for food, and Indigenous people for life? How thin can we spread the bounty? Does anyone have to give up their lifestyle altogether? Who gets to decide? And what will they say to those they erase?

Tonight we bring you some excerpts from that Town Hall meeting.

(*Characters speak to the group as well as to the audience. As each person speaks the others respond in character, sometimes audibly, to other characters' perspectives. Actors should work to listen in active ways that raise the stakes and the "heat" in the room. This public forum is not easy. We join the proceedings in progress.)*

WILL: All along the Klamath River we need to have the federal government recognize that tribes have a senior water right. That was in our treaties. We have court cases and court decisions that have substantiated this right. "How much water does it take to protect fish?" For crying out loud, enough so that they don't die. This is an allocation issue plain and simple. More water must flow downriver.

TIM: Look, I'm not anti-fish, I'm just anti-bullshit. I don't accept that the water is overallocated. My family has been cattle ranching in Upper Klamath for a hundred and fifty years. A lot of folks like me love this land as much as our Klamath and Modoc neighbors do. We're trying to preserve a way of life that has been handed down, and fight off the carnivorous southern California developers. We want to preserve our traditional rural values. We want our children to have a reason to stay and work the land. And that means economic incentives.

KLAMATH TRIBAL MEMBER/JOHNNY: (*to Tim*) You talk about your family values, man. We've seen evidence of your people's values over the years. Like when our reservation was "terminated" without our participation or consent. We were participating in your "economic incentives" back then in 1930, 1940, fair and square. Then in the 1950s your government just terminated our land—no democratic process, just took it. How many times you gonna take it, man? (pause) We not only lost our land, we lost our whole social fabric. Some of us lost our souls. I don't want that to happen to the Indian people in the Lower Klamath. That's all I got to say right now.

POLITICIAN: (*As she speaks, a PowerPoint slide show begins with an image of the Klamath watershed and then malfunctions as logos of dozens of regulatory agencies appear one on top of the other, blotting out the map of the Klamath watershed.*) I've represented folks in the Klamath region proudly for two terms now. You know, I was raised on a farm, looking out at those hills of waving green, learning the names of the birds that migrate through here. I think this is so wonderful that you all decided to come together to really talk through these issues. This is the democratic process at work! I think there's a lot we can do to help at the state and federal levels. The federal Bureau of Reclamation, the Bureau of Indian Affairs, the federal BM—BLM, and of course together with the state and federal fish and wildlife agencies, the Klamath Watershed Council, the National Forest Service, and the National Park Service, I think we can do a lot. I'll be working with my counterpart in the great state of California, together with folks from Del Norte County and the Yurok Rancheria, the Nine Feathered—uh, Federated Tribes of Oregon, especially the Klamath Tribes, you know really working with the good folks from Klamath County, Lake County, uh—and Harney County, Baker—all the good folks of my district here in Oregon, ready to commemorate—I mean collaborate with the folks in Trinity, Siskiyou, and Modoc Counties, and Del Norte—I mentioned Del Norte County—I did? Well, what I mean is working together is the way this country was built, settled, the way it was built, the way families are formed, and nations forged. So I'm glad you folks have come together, and with all these jurisdictions puttin' nose to the grindstone, I'm sure that we'll find a way to protect salmon and potatoes!

LOUISE: (*cutting her off*) You know what, my family have lived along that River for thousands of years—way before all those lines on the map were drawn, by the way. I've heard from a lot of folks from Klamath Falls who are ranchers or farmers, and they're like, "Geez, this is third generation for our family to be here." And I understand that, but it's like, this is the hundredth generation for my people, so put it in perspective. When the fish died, that was me, also dying. That was our people.

FISHERWOMAN: I live in Crescent City, California. My family business is fishing and we don't have any support from the government like you all. I drove up here because I wanna know how the hell a whole industry disappears overnight? Marine Fisheries Department tell us we're out of a job this year, next year. The seventies were hard enough, when we started feeling the effects of the dams. A lot of families got out. Now our worst nightmare has become reality. The whole coastline is closed. We've lost a whole industry in the blink of an eye without compensation or even much notice by the government. The effects on families are long term—the divorce rates, the domestic violence, the drunk driving rates. We sold our boat, Sonja, for seven thousand dollars, and that's what I been living on. My husband was aching to be back at sea. He lives by the elements—water, fish, and family. He went to Alaska to work crab 'cause there aren't any fish here. Crabbin's very dangerous if you know—(her voice breaks). My community will never get back what we've lost.

WALT: (*he is heartfelt, not aggressive*) My ancestors came from Eastern Europe, got out of the tenements of New York, then came to the Klamath Basin in nineteen-ought-two. The government wanted them to "feed the West" and said "we're gonna fund it." The Bureau of Reclamation was gonna build a dam and recover Tule Lake. My ancestors were part of a national dream. And then after World War II the government was giving land to veterans, and so it went for seventy years. Everything went pretty well until the Endangered Species Act passed. Now suing under the ESA has become a cottage industry out here thanks to a band of liberal-ass judges! I worked hard, all my life. I got up at four in the morning, hardly ever saw my children, built this farm, to grow what I was told would feed Americans. I resent being held to count by a bunch of lazy hippies and Indians. I tell you one thing, the farmers are the next Indians being run off their land by the government!

KLAMATH TRIBAL MEMBER: You just can't see how your way ruined our land. Two hundred seventy-five thousand acres of natural wetlands have been dried and turned to farmland to grow hay, alfalfa, potatoes, whatever. Cattle have trampled the sacred headwaters. The mistake goes back to when the US Bureau of Reclamation dried up the ancient homeland of the Modoc people—Tule and Klamath Lake; back to the broken treaty of 1864. You say, well that was a long time ago, but like she said, when your people have been on this land for tens of thousands of years, it's just yesterday, man.

ANDY: I grew up Karuk. I remember when I was seven years old I caught my first Salmon. I was so proud because now my family would have food to eat! There's a whole tradition with this place . . . you fasted and you prayed to get the spring chinook to come early . . . it's no different than your Christian faith. You've prayed for rain, haven't you? I've heard some things today that . . . I need to say this. I need to dispel this myth of the lazy Indian. There's a lot of work going on here . . . the basket making and making the nets and tending the trees and doing control burns to clear the undergrowth—this River is a garden! These stereotypes are dangerous. We have an elder here who just passed away. He signed up and fought for this country in World War II, and then when he came back, the US Forest Service had sold off his land. The Karuk have chosen not to fish the spring runs anymore because they're so low—and no EPA ruling had to tell us that! We know how to manage this resource.

WHITE-WATER GUIDE: I run Blue Mountain Rafting Company where the Salmon River meets the Klamath. (*to WALT*) I used to be a hippie, by the way. (*then to everyone*) The year of the fish kill there was so little water that we had to shut down. It wasn't safe. No jet boats, no rafts. That summer I saw rocks that I didn't know existed before! We are part of this community too. We uphold part of the economy here. We care about the health of this river. We want to see it free and wild and runnable for our grandchildren and yours. We've got to ask, what's our ethical obligation here? Doesn't our ethical obligation outweigh even the economic concerns? Sure, farmers are going to have to take a hit—we have, the tribes have—we all have to share in the change because it's the right thing to do for this extraordinary wilderness. You'd sacrifice for your child, if your child was sick. It's a sacrifice, but it's also an act of love.

JULIE: She's right. This is a community issue, not just an Indian issue. Most non-Natives see it that way, and they don't even understand what that means. It's a spiritual issue for all of us. It's our job to take responsibility. We have an opportunity to right a great wrong here.

PRIEST: I want to follow up—if I may? As you see, I'm nobody's enemy here. I've been at St. Joseph's parish for, what, four years now?

I'm just beginning to understand how deep these issues are, and I respect everybody's view and the stake you all have in this. But like she said, there's a time when we all have to sacrifice. And sometimes what we have to sacrifice is our pride, and our anger. I grew up in Pasadena. I had no idea where Klamath Falls was when I got assigned, but when I looked on a map—I was standing in the dining room with my mother and my grandmother—and I said, hey, there's a lake near there—Tule Lake. My grandmother—and this is a tough little Japanese woman, you know—she never cries. She went out of the room, into the bedroom, and my mom followed her. I was like, what's wrong with grandma? I'd heard a few stories, but mostly what I knew about the Japanese internment camps was from school—history of World War II, all that. That day I found out that my grandfather died in the internment camp at Tule Lake. So there's blood for me here too, you see. Forgiveness does not mean that we forget, or that we don't hurt, or that the ghosts go away. It just means that we do our business from a different place in our hearts—that we are willing to conduct ourselves with the good of all our neighbors on our minds. That's the way we honor the ones who came before.

(Town Hall assumes frozen or slow-motion position and silence, while lights change to show TIM has gone outside to look for BEN/GRACE; he runs into JULIE heading for the ladies' room with her baby in a traditional cradleboard.)

JULIE: Hey.

TIM: Lookin' for my son [daughter], he [she] got kinda antsy in there.

JULIE: I know the feeling.

TIM: He's [She's] ten. Hey, thank you for what you said in there. I guess I never saw it that way. (*She is about to walk past him, then stops.*)

JULIE: What's your son's [daughter's] name?

TIM: Ben [Grace]. He's [She's] ten. I said that. My mother used to tell me that I slept in a baby basket like that.

JULIE: Really?

TIM: How old is she, about twelve months?

JULIE: Eight months.

TIM: She's beautiful. Babies are like little ambassadors from another world!

JULIE: They are.

TIM: Yeah. (*pause*) So, do you think we'll solve anything here?

JULIE: I doubt it. I've heard a lot of this talk before.

TIM: So what would help?

JULIE: I don't know. I guess if people up there understood that this is not only our livelihood that's at stake, it's our culture, our traditions, our way of life.

TIM: People where I come from think they are trying to protect their way of life too.

JULIE: Tell that to my father and her dad when seventy thousand salmon lie rotting on the riverbank!

TIM: Okay.

JULIE: Okay what?

TIM: Okay, I'd like to listen to them, your dad and your husband and whoever will . . . I guess . . .

(*BEN [GRACE] comes from around a corner.*)

BEN/GRACE: Yo, Dad!

TIM: Where'd you run off to?

BEN/GRACE: I met this guy . . .

TIM: Ben [Grace], this is Julie.

BEN/GRACE: Hey. Dad, do we have to go back in there?

(*back inside the Town Hall*)

(*In the following monologue, KATE is referring to the same place that ROSE has just described—the mouth of the Klamath River at Requa. About halfway through her monologue, as KATE moves downstage and speaks increasingly to the audience, the lights in the house, or audience portion of the theatre, may slowly come up, allowing KATE to see the audience, and audience members to see one another.*)

KATE: The mouth of the Klamath is a glorious place, the River rushing out into the sea. As I walk the beach with my friends whose families fish there, they're all "Can I borrow your binoculars? I wanna see who's down there. I wanna see who's eeling. Check it out!" Some guys on a quad are zooming by and they're whistling and asking if we want a ride and my friends are all "oh, those guys," and "yeah, they're cousins, we're so over them." And then it hits me! I'm out here like this is some wild coastal preserve; but my friends are in their neighborhood. This is their hood! Where they hang in summer; where they meet guys and dance and sleep over and eat food that their moms made and where they play radios loud and tell secrets to girlfriends. And then it hit me again. What if, in your neighborhood, in mine, at the end of a fabulous summer, there were seventy thousand dead animals on the streets, in the yards, on the sidewalk, animals you loved, animals you knew and considered part of your family? Animals that were the lifeblood of your community? What if that happened to you? And it began to sink in, what this meant, what it must have felt like, just a little. (*exits through audience*)

(*cross fade to REPORTER*)

REPORTER: Ladies and gentlemen, we're going to take a ten-minute break now. There are some refreshments and exhibits about the salmon and the Klamath River in the lobby. This might be a good time to meet your neighbors. (*exits through audience, as lights come up*)

{ INTERMISSION }

ACT TWO

SCENE 13–HIP-HOP

Outside Town Hall as in scene 12. WILL, ZEEK, LITTLE MARY listening to hip-hop on WILL's iPod with earpiece. Audience coming back into the theatre from intermission should also hear the music.

ZEEK: Cool. I wanna get one.

LITTLE MARY: I want to listen. Let me listen too!

WILL: Here. No, put it on like this.

LITTLE MARY: I know how to do it!

ZEEK: No she doesn't.

WILL: Hey, whatever. She's got it.

(*Little Mary dances to the music.*)

ZEEK: Oh man . . .

WILL: Leave her be. I'd like to see you do some moves!

(*They notice BEN [GRACE] on the other side listening, watching.*)

WILL: Yo, dude, come on over! You can hang with us. Get outa that meeting.

BEN/GRACE: I got one (*shows iPod*). It needs charging.

ZEEK: He raps.

BEN/GRACE: You rap?

WILL: I do.

BEN/GRACE: Cool.

ZEEK: Go on, Uncle Will, do the rap you made about the Salmon.

WILL: Nah . . .

LITTLE MARY: Yeah, do the one . . . Do it! Pleeeeaaase, Uncle Will.

ZEEK: Chill, dude!

WILL: (*performs an original rap number; children dance; laughter, etc. Children cheer and applaud when WILL is finished.*)

BEN/GRACE: That was cool!

WILL: You got any moves?

BEN/GRACE: Some.

(ZEEK and LITTLE MARY do some hip-hop; BEN [GRACE] does a version.)

WILL: Okay, okay . . . You got a unique style!

BEN/GRACE: I think I gotta find my Dad.

WILL: Thanks for hangin'.

ZEEK: See ya.

(BEN [GRACE] exits. Transition lighting. The sound of RACHEL singing can overlap the end of the scene, taking us into the next scene.)

SCENE 14–TIRES

Pool of light on RACHEL as she begins the prayers and movements of Shabbat and lights candles, a loaf of bread before her.

RACHEL: *Baruk ata adonoi elohanu / Mela ha olam . . .*

(KATE enters, drops gear and backpack, then stubs her toe.)

KATE: Crap. Sorry. Sorry I'm late. I can never remember what time you start this.

RACHEL: Sundown.

KATE: That's not a time.

RACHEL: It used to be a time.

KATE: I really need to take a shower. (*taking off layers of outdoor clothing*)

RACHEL: In the cycle of the seasons, in sacred time, sundown is a time, a time that the people understood as a time.

KATE: But not six o'clock?

RACHEL: No, that's western rational time.

KATE: Not sacred time.

RACHEL: Are we gonna do this again?

KATE: I just need a time, that's all.

RACHEL: That's the point, you can't program Shabbat into your cell phone. It's not that kind of time.

KATE: Sorry. Really I am.

RACHEL: You of all people should know that there are different kinds of time—there is the time the salmon come home in the fall, the time the salmon come home in the spring. Isn't that what you're trying to get the farmers and feds up there to understand?

KATE: That's political.

RACHEL: It's spiritual. If you miss that, I don't think all your biological opinions are worth much. (*pause*) So, how was it?

KATE: Sure is gorgeous country. When you come over this ridge, there it is, the basin—the war zone—but it looked like heaven. Then I start noticing the signs. Like "Farmers Feed America," "Forget the Fish and Feed the Masses," "EPA Go Home," or "I'm pro Farmer, I vote *and* I shoot." Oh, you were right about the bumper sticker, by the way.

RACHEL: Did you talk to anyone?

KATE: Park rangers. Agency biologists. You know me, I don't know how. You don't just walk up to someone with pointy boots in a feed store and say, "Hey, are you a farmer or a rancher? Are you running twelve thousand head of Angus on land that used to belong to the Klamath Tribes? Or are you a farmer growing monsoon crops in what used to be, and incidentally still is, seasonal wetlands? Can we talk?" No I didn't talk to anyone. Well, no, I did talk to one guy. But not about fish. I had a few close encounters . . .

RACHEL: What—?

KATE: . . . of the redneck kind. I didn't talk to anyone, Rach, because I was in getting coffee at this mom-and-pop diner and somebody, some buckaroo, some bucket-brigadier was out in broad daylight slashing my tires.

RACHEL: Oh my God! Are you okay? (*spoken simultaneously with KATE's next line*)

(*Lights change as she enters the scene; TIM joins her. KATE, coming out of a diner with coffee, sees her car. TIM is on his way in. He sees it too.*)

KATE: Oh my God. Oh my God.

TIM: Ouch!

KATE: (*turns on TIM*) Who did this? Did you see them? What kind of people do this? (*takes out cell phone*) I'm calling the police. Shit. (*Her phone is out of range.*) Why did they do this? Who are they? Where am I?!

TIM: It happens. You're in Klamath Falls. Take it easy. Let's get you some help. (*takes out his cell phone*) Bob. Tim. Busy? Good. Would you send a truck over to Maxine's parking lot with a couple of tires for a—(*He walks around car.*)

KATE: Toyota Corolla—

TIM: Nineteen—

KATE: 1998.

TIM: 1998. No, that's okay. I'll be gone, but just take care of it for me, okay? (*offers her his phone*) Here, wanna call the police?

KATE: Yeah. What's the number up here?

TIM: 911, I think.

KATE: Oh man, this is gonna max out my Visa.

TIM: Tires are on me.

KATE: What? No. No way! You can't do that.

TIM: Too late, already did. I'm sorry about this.

KATE: It wasn't your fault.

TIM: No, but it's my town.

KATE: Who did this? Why?

TIM: People do stupid things when they feel powerless. They see your bumper sticker and, well, it's a guerrilla war for them. Like Captain

Jack fighting off the US Cavalry to hold on to the Modoc homelands. A lot of these farmers and ranchers think they're Captain Jack now. "I'm pro Salmon and I vote"? That's cute. Well, I gotta get to the feed store, got a sick calf. Bob will fix you up.

KATE: Wait. Thanks. Uh, I'm Kate.

TIM: Tim. Tim McNeil.

KATE: Thanks.

(*Transition suggested through lighting, imagery, and/or sound.*)

SCENE 15–THE VISIT*

Location same as scene 2. JULIE and WILL at home.

JULIE: Just try to be civil, okay? He wants to hear our perspective, that's all.

WILL: You didn't answer my question. Who said you could invite this guy to our home?

JULIE: No one. No one said. No one needed to say who I can invite.

WILL: This is your Gram's house, and you didn't ask her? And you sure as hell didn't ask me.

(*knock at the door*)

JULIE: Please, Will, just one cup of coffee? (*She answers the door.*)

TIM: (*enters*) Hi. You must be Will. (*an awkward moment*)

JULIE: How was your drive? Did you come through Happy Camp or around?

TIM: Around. I never get to see enough of the ocean.

JULIE: Then you drove along the Smith River, before Crescent City. Did you stop at Requa like I told you?

TIM: I did. I hiked to the top where you can look down on the mouth.

* Portions of WILL's dialogue are adapted from "Fish Kill: For the Yurok, Salmon Is Everything" by Barry McCovey Jr.

JULIE: That's near where we have our Brush Dances.

TIM: Beautiful country. Beautiful river.

WILL: Should have seen it when there were thousands of dead fish floating on top.

TIM: I'm sorry that happened. I know it was real hard on your family and your people.

JULIE: Want coffee?

WILL: No. No. I'm sorry. Mr. uh—

TIM: McNeil.

WILL: Mr. McNeil. This is our "people's" house—our Gram who didn't speak for four days after the fish kill. Julie's father whose only work this season has been counting the dead.

TIM: I'm just trying to understand the implications . . .

WILL: (*to JULIE*) What is this? Another "study"? (*to TIM*) You don't have the stomach for the implications, man. This is genocide going on here. Like killing off the buffalo. Only now we recognize the pattern.

TIM: I don't think . . .

WILL: Now you come down here like we're all supposed to sit around some Thanksgiving table and what, eat potatoes?

JULIE: He doesn't grow potatoes.

WILL: Well, I don't want your poison food. I don't want to sit at your table. I want you to get—

JULIE: Will, please.

TIM: That's okay. I want to hear what he has to say.

WILL: I've lived in the Klamath River system my entire life. The River is part of me, the lifeblood of my people. . . . The Klamath is my home, my church, garden, highway, counselor, friend, brother—hell, provider. . . . The carnage I've seen over the weeks is so utterly disgusting I can't sleep. I close my eyes and the images of dead, rotting fish—maybe you've seen photographs . . . but you cannot begin to imagine the smell. The smell of death and decay messes with my mind. I can't eat because food, no matter what it is, reminds me of the smell. Come walk along the banks of the River with me . . . I dare you . . . Come and walk with me and cut open the bellies of rotten salmon to detect their sex . . . Come and walk with me . . . count with me . . . hack their tails so they won't be recounted. You can't escape the smell. This is a real-life situation. It's not a book; it's not pretend. It's not something you read about that happened a hundred years ago. It's happening right now, today. To people in my life. Maybe all your rancher and farmer friends up there don't understand that. You tell them to get the hell down here and help us clean up this mess that they helped make. (*pause*) That's all I have to say.

TIM: I will tell them. (*WILL leaves.*)

JULIE: I'm sorry.

TIM: No, don't be. I'm glad he spoke his mind. I wanted to hear.

JULIE: We aren't asking for all the water, just enough for Salmon to survive. . . . Salmon are the center of our culture. If they leave the River, we don't know what will become of us. . . . We are running out of miracles.

TIM: I know. Us too. Thanks for havin' me down.

(*Transition suggested through lighting, imagery, and/or sound.*)

SCENE 16–RANCH TOUR*

TIM's office in Upper Klamath region, near Chiloquin. KATE enters.

KATE: I didn't know ranchers had offices.

TIM: It's a business.

KATE: Yeah. Guess I expected moose heads on the wall, and, well, you know, big bear hide rugs.

TIM: Those are at the house.

* The story told by KATE in the middle of the scene was originally told to me by Jean O'Hara and Jessica Eden; details have been changed.

KATE: Thanks for meeting me. I don't really know where to begin. There's a lot of people in pain where I live, tribal people who depend on Salmon for subsistence, commercial fishermen and women who lost their livelihood. They think you all up here are using all the water and not enough goes downriver.

TIM: Wanna see some birds, or are you just a fish person?

KATE: No. No, I like birds.

TIM: Our ranch is a historic wetland, so we can't just put all the water in-stream for the suckerfish, or any fish. We'd lose the wetlands, we'd lose the sandhill crane.

KATE: Seasonal wetlands actually. . . . The birds use the wetlands when nature makes wetlands—in the winter and spring. "Preserving" wetlands in the middle of summer with irrigation, when the fish need the water, is kinda over-management.

(*walking outside*)

TIM: People up here are just scared, Kate. A lot went down during the time of Termination.

KATE: The fifties?

TIM: Yes, and before and after. Klamath tribal land used to extend "from mountain top to mountain top." Then came the Dawes Act that tried to make Indians into farmers. Whites like my great-grandfather started buyin' up allotments; that's how we came by these acres. Then in the 1950s the federal government terminated the last of the Klamath Reservation. That brought a stampede of social problems, the drugs, alcohol, wrecked cars, and wrecked homes. We have so much conflict in our community it's just hard to see the bigger picture. We have a history of violence at a level no one talks about. There's a lot of shame around it. We made a lot of mistakes, but I think you'll find when you really listen that people up here do care about the land, about each other. We keep the cattle outa the riparian areas; we try to do right by our Indian neighbors. You met Phillip—he's a good friend to my family, but my father almost killed his father forty years ago. Things change.

KATE: My friend and I were traveling through Idaho a couple years ago coming back from a ski trip, and we stopped in this diner for hot fudge sundaes. A group of skinheads came in, shaved head, swastika tattoos, the whole bit. They started checking us out, you know, and I looked at my friend, my girlfriend, we both had spiked hair then, and I thought, "Do we look queer . . . and how Jewish does she look?" I live in a town where I can hold her hand in line at the post office. But there we were in Idaho and cold fear just shot through me. When I saw my tires that day, I had the same feeling. It didn't hit me that it was about fish.

TIM: What's your girlfriend's name?

KATE: Rachel.

TIM: Is she a fish lady too?

KATE: No, she's a photographer and rabbi-wannabe.

TIM: Bring her up, take pictures. We get a lot of photographers up here. My son's favorite subject is the pelican. Look at those guys! Makes you wonder what God was thinking.

KATE: She's the one told me to come back and talk to you. She has this theory—she's kind of a new-age Jew—about how the universe is like one big garment, that all the violence and distrust in the world are like tears in the fabric and that all we can do with our lives is try to mend little bits of the garment.

TIM: We're trying. Some of us are trying to mend what our ancestors broke. But we can't do it if we're being shot at.

(*KATE and TIM take a moment, shake hands, exit different directions. Cross fade.*)

SCENE 17–COMMUNION*

Location same as scene 3. In the Catholic tradition of ensuring that those who cannot attend Mass receive Holy Communion, the parish PRIEST has come to visit ALICE to hear her confession and serve Communion to her.

PRIEST: . . . Forgive us our trespasses as we forgive those who trespass against us. Lead us not into temptation, but deliver us from evil.

ALICE: Amen.

PRIEST: Deliver us from every evil, oh Lord . . .

BOTH: For Yours is the kingdom and the power and the glory now and forever. Amen.

PRIEST: (*takes a Host from a small gold compact*) Alice, the body of Christ.

ALICE: Amen. (*She takes the Host, eats, makes sign of the cross; pauses in prayer while PRIEST puts his compact and religious items away. ALICE makes the sign of the cross again and then lifts her head.*)

ALICE: Thank you, Father. Coffee's hot.

PRIEST: Cookies in the regular place?

ALICE: Yep, unless Ben [Grace] got to 'em. Help yourself.

(*slight pause as he looks offstage for cookies and gets cup of coffee, and ALICE reflects*)

ALICE: In my mind it was all about coming to this place, the natural beauty, and fixing the River. Fixing everything. Showing, in some way, with an angry determination, that really agriculture and rivers could live together. The opportunities to change the place were unlimited. Drag tires and washers out of the spring. Paint the old dingy house. Move cattle from here to there and then back over here. Don't let them eat the new willows. Fence the River. Dig thistles. Clean the shop. Chainsaw down the old fence, build some new fence. Bring

* Portions of ALICE's lines are adapted from "Yainix Journal" by Becky Hatfield Hyde and inspired by Yainix Ranch; details have been fictionalized.

people together. Change the place. The hardest realization for me is that what's really changing is me. This is a bit unsettling for someone controlling enough to think that they might change a place, a valley of rushes and sedges and people!

TIM: (*as he enters*) Change it and hope that someone like the environmental community would notice and let rural communities survive. Hey, Father, how are you?

PRIEST: Doin' the doing of the Lord. (*laughs*)

ALICE: You like that line, don't you, Father?

TIM: Well, I'm grateful somebody's doin' it!

PRIEST: Indeed. (*pause*) Well, gotta head up to see Phillip's aunt next. Thanks for the cookies.

TIM: Thanks for coming, Father.

PRIEST: See you next time. (*exits*)

(*slight pause while TIM takes off jacket, gets coffee, or other business*)

TIM: Ran into Phillip at the cash machine that night of Ben's baseball [Grace's softball] game. We were all standing there in the Bank of America parking lot looking up at the stars. Ben [Grace] was asking if we could see the Milky Way . . .

(*Lighting change; PHILLIP is seen, and then joins them, as TIM's memory becomes the present.*)

BEN/GRACE: Where's the Big Dipper again?

TIM: See that star there, follow my finger. Right there, just over home plate.

BEN/GRACE: I see it! Cool.

TIM: Now listen. Keep your eye on my finger. See the Dipper's four corners? Now follow the handle and then up—that's the North Star! That's what the first explorers used to navigate to the New World.

BEN/GRACE: The North Star's not very bright.

TIM: But it's constant. That's why ships could navigate by it.

BEN/GRACE: What about GPS?

TIM: Before GPS, silly!

BEN/GRACE: So, why do they call it the Milky Way? Does the Dipper get milk out of it?

PHILLIP: We call it "where the people come home." All the ancestors are up there, watching over you, and dancing with you.

(*Lighting transition back to ALICE and TIM; PHILLIP exits.*)

TIM: Now every time he [she] sees the Milky Way he [she] does this hip-hop move and says, "Yo, I am dancin' with the ancestors!"

ALICE: I was never a very good dancer.

TIM: Me neither.

(*Transition suggested through lighting, imagery, and/or sound.*)

SCENE 18–CAPTAIN JACK'S STRONGHOLD

The craggy landscape of Lava Beds National Monument suggested in light or projections. TIM sits alone, fingering a brochure; then speaks directly to audience.

TIM: If you're a tourist at Lava Beds National Monument you pass General Canby's marker first—a white cross at the place he breathed his last, after Captain Jack's ambush. Looking north just there you can see the southern boundary of my brother's acreage in the Tule Lake sump. This is sagebrush. High desert. Seasonal wetland. You drive up another three miles into the weird lava formations and there's another little interpretive area called Captain Jack's Stronghold. In 1873 fifty-one Modoc warriors held up right here and fought off the US Army. Fifty-one warriors killed upwards of four hundred cavalrymen. Look around, you can see what a great fortress the land provided. (*takes out tobacco as if to roll a cigarette*) Black lava rocks in mounds that would allow fellas to hide easy. A few juniper pines, lots of sagebrush, crevices where a whole line of men could hide and still see and shoot anybody approaching from the low-lying marshes. Fifty-one warriors and their families spent a whole winter here and the army couldn't take 'em. Tule Lake used to come right up to the edge of this high ground. Finally the army was able to cut off the Indians' access to water. All the Modocs wanted . . . you can read about it in the little trail guide . . . all Captain Jack wanted was for his people "to live unmolested on their homeland." They just wanted to be safe, just like me, just like you. (*respectfully, in manner of the Native people he knows, throws some tobacco on the ground in prayer*)

(*Transition suggested through lighting, imagery, and/or sound.*)

SCENE 19–ULTIMATE TITLE*

Same as scene 3. Light fades up on rancher's family. Outside, looking out over the Klamath Marsh from the large porch of a ranch house built in 1890s. Sounds of wildlife. ALICE and TIM on their porch looking out over the marsh they irrigate and the land on which they run cattle, the same land that belonged to the Klamath Tribe "from mountain top to mountain top."

TIM: (*sitting on the stoop, rolling a cigarette*) Moon's not up yet.

ALICE: Nope.

(*pause, then a splash*)

TIM: Hear that? Owl got himself a bullfrog.

ALICE: Guess he'll live for one more day.

TIM: Don't brood, Mom, it's too cold for that.

ALICE: A woman prays for sons when she marries land like this. Don't have 'em and you feel like you failed the land. Now I got 'em . . .

TIM: You didn't fail, none of us failed.

ALICE: My eldest son suing my youngest son, taking away the only

* Portions of ALICE's lines are adapted from "Yainix Journal" by Becky Hatfield Hyde and inspired by Yainix Ranch; details have been fictionalized. For more information, see Ann Adams, "Investing in a Sustainable Future: Yainix Ranch," *Holistic Management in Practice*, July/August 2005, 5–6; and Mary Christina Wood and Zachary Welcker, "Tribes as Trustees Again (Part I): The Emerging Tribal Role in Conservation Trust Movement," *Harvard Environmental Law Review* 32:1 (2008): 373–432. The story told by PHILLIP was originally told to me by Marlon Sherman.

peace I've ever had, and you tell me we got only three options: give in to Greg and lose our water, sell to these vulture developers, or do this so-called land trust arrangement with the Indians. None of those sound like the American dream to me. If I can't die knowing my great-grandchildren are going to inherit this, going to continue on this land, my life might as well be dust, just like my Gramma's. She died with a mouthful of Kansas dust.

TIM: I know, Mom. Nobody's leaving. Just the paperwork is changing. It's like you always said, God's got Ultimate Title.

ALICE: We ran three thousand head of Angus once we got the last allotment. Three thousand head. Then okay, we gotta be careful of erosion and fouling the water; okay, we run fewer and fewer head. But damn it, we're hardly making it now. And now my other son the potato farmer is taking what's left. What will be left for my grandchildren?

TIM: Change happens, Mom.

(*pause*)

ALICE: One December Gregory got so sick that along with a temperature of a hundred and three his heart rate was two hundred, and below his breastbone was contracting in several inches every time he took a breath. . . . By the time we finally got to the emergency room his black curls were wet with sweat and stuck to his head. Gave him fluids, antibiotics. . . . By the time we got checked out of the hospital, I got the flu and couldn't talk. When we got home neighbors showed up . . . made soup; figured out the dosing schedule for his five medications. They walked the baby—that was you. You were a very fussy baby.

(*PHILLIP is seen in a pool of light upstage, carrying a traditional cradleboard.*)

One day when Phillip was over, you were fussing. The next Sunday, Phillip returned with a baby basket made specially to fit you.

TIM: I didn't know Phillip made it—for me.

ALICE: It's soft leather on the front with laces that crisscross up the front.

PHILLIP: The frame is made of hazelwood.

ALICE: The back is soft black leather. Inside is a hand-sewn corduroy pillow. You slept sound in your cradleboard; your eyes would open, and then shut, your little face smiling. (*pause*) How does one put into words the special nature of such a gift? How does one begin to give back?

TIM: We just start, I guess.

ALICE: (*stands and walks forward a step or two as if seeing the image)* I know what it's like when the sandhill cranes return to the Sycan Marsh—a marsh we irrigate. It's like a miracle. Miles of silver shining wings. A visitation of spirit. I'd grab you and little Greg and say, "Look! There they are! The good Lord sent the cranes back to us again!" (*pause*) But I don't know what it's like when the Salmon return.

TIM: We can imagine. (*stands beside her*) We can imagine what it might be like to have those Salmon returning, not just to the Klamath River, but to the Sycan River. I can feel the excitement for what it might be like to have them come. To be a hungry seven-year-old boy—and have them come.

ALICE: I am tired of fighting. I am hungry in my soul. I suppose it would be more an act of love than of water. Holding another place tight, holding other families tight. Love is the only thing that ever changes anything anyway.

(*BEN [GRACE] has come out to join them, sleepy.*)

TIM: Couldn't sleep?

ALICE: What's the matter, Bunny?

BEN/GRACE: Are we going to give our land back to the Indians, Dad?

ALICE: Bunny, no . . .

BEN/GRACE: Gram . . . sheesh. What's a Conservation Land Trust? Do we have to move?

TIM: No, no. We can live here as long as we want. It just means that we're going to work with our Indian neighbors to help take care of the land. It's kinda like what Phillip said, like when you're dancing with the ancestors.

BEN/GRACE: Are you going to dance? I'd like to see that! C'mon, Dad, let's see some moves!

TIM: I'm going to try. You teach me?

BEN/GRACE: Nah . . . but I met this guy at that Town Hall thing. . . . He raps . . . and it was really cool and . . .

TIM: Okay, okay, up to bed with you. (*They exit.*)

(*Transition suggested through lighting, imagery, and/or sound.*)

SCENE 20–SACRED IS*

Location same as scene 10. The entire scene is ceremonial in tone. The SALMON DANCER joins at some point.

ROSE: (*speaking as the River*) When I was a child, the River gave me a prayer: "I am alive in you and I am the source of your hope. Every time someone appreciates my stillness, my beauty and peace, eats the food that I offer, cares for the vegetation and the wild animals that I sustain—every moment of your gratefulness is my renewal."

LOUISE: Sacred were gifts that were given to us by Creator at that time of the spirit people.

JULIE: Sacred is a word that if said in the Yurok language would likely have so much more meaning than in English. In this language it doesn't do justice to my life or my people.

ROSE: Sacred is the stories that we were given from our elders, who learned them from their elders. Sacred is our prayer medicine that carries my prayers, hopes, and dreams up to Creator every night. Our ceremonies are sacred and bring life, repairing bad feelings or wrong actions.

LOUISE: Sacred is my relative, the Salmon, who has ensured the survival of my people since time immemorial.

* Portions of this scene were adapted from reflective writings of Heather Hostler, Nikolai Colegrove, Lauren Taylor, Holly Couling, Ron Griffith, and Jessica Eden.

JULIE: Sacred is my family who love and support me and have given me the gift of self-respect.

LOUISE: Sacred is my daughter, without whom my life stops.

ROSE: Sacred is something woven into your life and the lives of your ancestors. It is something that can't be taken from you. Sacred is the Salmon, you need to protect it, because it protects you. Once the Salmon thrived and we prayed for them and gave them thanks as a whole tribe. We felt that it was our responsibility to take care of them, because they took care of us. Now, we struggle with wanting to do something, but feeling helpless. I don't believe this means it is lost. It is an opportunity to bring back something that has been done since time before time. We need to once again take care of the Salmon physically and spiritually. This is the time, for their survival and ours.

(*The recorded voices of "Sacred Is . . ." in Klamath, Yurok, Hupa, Karuk, and English mingle with the live voices; we lose the English and finally hear only the Indigenous languages, which continue under ROSE's lines and TIM and JULIE's phone conversation.*)

(*TIM alone; visibly moved; he takes out a cell phone, looks up a number, and dials. JULIE's phone rings and she picks up and steps away; the others freeze.*)

JULIE: Iye-ah-qui!

TIM: Julie? Hi. Tim McNeil.

JULIE: Hi.

TIM: Hope I didn't catch you at a bad time. How are you?

JULIE: Keepin' on keepin' on.

TIM: Listen, I don't know how to say this . . . but I wanted to say something . . . I mean I want to do something, we're trying to do something up here, but it's going to take some time. . . . You know how you were telling me about how when the first salmon came up the river that your people would do a ceremony and then send a runner upriver to the Karuks and Nu-Tini-Xwes and then they would do a ceremony?

JULIE: Yeah—

(JULIE can respond with "uh huh" or "okay" or other utterances during the following monologue as she begins to understand TIM's plan.)

TIM: I know this sounds stupid, but when that first salmon comes I want you to call me. Call me and tell me, okay? Would you do that? And on that day I'm going to go down to the pivot field and turn off my irrigation for the day. And if the main pump is running, I'll turn it off too. Then, we're going to call our friends who irrigate down in the Scott Valley and they're going to turn their pumps off. And I'm going to call Walt in the Klamath Project and he's agreed to turn his water off for a day. And he's going to call the members of the Water Users Association and they're all gonna turn their water off on that day. A dozen admin folks who work for the City of Klamath Falls are going to fill milk jugs with water from the tap in their house and drive it down to the edge of the Klamath River and dump it in. Don't laugh. I know it's more an act of love than of water. It's holding another place tight, holding other families tight.

JULIE: Okay.

TIM: Okay?

JULIE: Okay. I'll call you. I'll tell my Gram and the others.

TIM: This is just a start. We've got a lot of people up here that'll be tough to convince because they're afraid.

JULIE: I always wonder if the Salmon are afraid after they've gotten used to the ocean and all that freedom, if they're afraid to swim home.

TIM: Well, I hope we can all have as much courage as a fish.

(SALMON DANCER moves more freely among and around the women as cross fade to REPORTER.)

REPORTER: Here in the Upper Klamath, some say a handful of farmers and ranchers have lost their marbles. What will one day of water do for the salmon struggling up the Klamath? Spokespersons say that this show of solidarity with fish and tribal people will be symbolic at first, but that others who hear the news will do what they can, in their way, on that day, when the fish come back.

ROSE: (*walking forward, again ceremonial*) When I was a child, the River gave me a prayer: "I am alive in you and I am the source of your hope. Every time someone appreciates my stillness, my beauty and peace, eats the food that I offer, cares for the vegetation and the wild animals that I sustain—every moment of your gratefulness is my renewal."

LOUISE: Sacred were gifts that were given to us by Creator at that time of the spirit people.

JULIE: Sacred is the stories that we were given from our elders.

ROSE: Sacred is our prayer medicine.

ZEEK: Sacred is my relative, the Salmon.

(*Others actors enter and join in, whispering "Sacred is . . . (family, river, land)" until all actors are onstage.*)

JULIE: Sacred is my family.

ALICE: Sacred is my family.

JOHNNY: Sacred is the River.

TIM: Sacred is the land that we steward.

BEN/GRACE: Sacred is my dad, and friends.

LOUISE: Sacred is my daughter, without whom my life stops.

LITTLE MARY: Sacred is the Salmon. We need to protect it because it protects us.

PHILLIP: It's all been said.

(*The voices of "Sacred Is . . ." in Klamath, Yurok, Karuk, and Hupa overlap the lines above; then finally only the recorded voices are heard as the lights dim. The voices continue for several seconds while the actors stand in darkness. Curtain or blackout.*)

When possible, performances should be followed by a community discussion, facilitated by local tribal leaders, elders, or others with an understanding of the issues.

ALTERNATE CHARACTERS FOR TOWN HALL, SCENE 12:

Depending on the desires of the production crew, the following characters and monologues may be substituted for two others, switching out, for example, WHITE-WATER GUIDE for one of these.

LOWER KLAMATH WOMAN: I'm from the Lower Klamath area. My father came to the redwoods down near the Smith River after the Vietnam War—he tried looking for Bigfoot and some gold mining with a pan . . . did logging till he got injured . . . taught him a lesson, he said "booze and chainsaws don't mix." Then went back to the woods where all the Vets live and . . . he couldn't live in the city . . . redwoods have a healing power, you know. That's why so many Vets come here to live in the woods. It's not just to grow Mary Jane . . . it's their home . . . I always like how Indian people introduce themselves and know where they came from, and it made me think about my great, great, great, great—that might be too many greats—grandmother, who was a slave. She got spirited to freedom on the Underground Railroad to San Francisco. It's bizarre to me to think about there was a time when slavery was legal in this country. But now it's not. Things change. It takes a long time to heal that stuff. But things do change. I want to say that Indians have something to teach us, something about caring for the places where we live, the places that protect us. And we might look back in a hundred years and think, gosh, they were right.

TEACHER: I live in Chiloquin. I am the daughter of a rancher and my husband is Klamath/Modoc. There are some folks on my side of the family won't even talk to his side of the family. My husband is angry. My father is angry. No one wants to leave this land. My son hunts and fishes. My daughter dances. And they have fun on the ranch too. This is not old ways versus new ways; it's not us versus them—this is us versus us. This is about who we are as a community.

Above: Marlon Sherman and Kathleen McCovey during rehearsal for the 2006 production of *Salmon Is Everything* at Humboldt State.
PHOTO: KELLIE BROWN

Left: Scene 2, "Salmon Is Family." Left to right: Julie (Shayleen Macy EagleSpeaker), Rose (Marta Lu Clifford), and Will (Kunu Dittmer) in the 2011 production of *Salmon Is Everything* at the University of Oregon.
PHOTO: ARIEL OGDEN

Lower Left: Scene 7, "Tourists." Left to right: Tourists (Christine Madzik and Joseph Gilg) and Julie (Shayleen Macy EagleSpeaker) in the 2011 production of *Salmon Is Everything* at the University of Oregon.
PHOTO: ARIEL OGDEN

Scene 12, "Town Hall." Louise (Ada Ball) and Julie (Shayleen Macy EagleSpeaker) in the 2011 production of *Salmon Is Everything* at the University of Oregon.
PHOTO: ARIEL OGDEN

Scene 13, "Hip-Hop." Ben (Rafael Halevy) and Little Mary (Ariana Sanchez) in the 2011 production of *Salmon Is Everything* at the University of Oregon.
PHOTO: ARIEL OGDEN

Scene 15, "The Visit." Rachel (Beth Weissbart) and Rose (Kathleen McCovey) in the 2006 production of *Salmon Is Everything* at Humboldt State University.
PHOTO: KELLIE BROWN

Scene 10, "Aftermath." Left to right: Kate (Darcie Beeman-Black) and Rachel (Beth Weissbart) in the 2006 production of *Salmon Is Everything* at Humboldt State University.
PHOTO: KELLIE BROWN

Scene 12, "Town Hall." Left to right: Johnny (Bobbie Perez), Kate (Darcie Beeman-Black), and Rachel (Beth Weissbart) in the 2006 production of *Salmon Is Everything* at Humboldt State University.
PHOTO: KELLIE BROWN

Mary Campbell as Julie in the 2006 production of *Salmon Is Everything* at Humboldt State University.
PHOTO: KELLIE BROWN

Scene 12, "Town Hall." Walt (Joseph Gilg), Louise (Ada Ball), Johnny (Richie Scott), and Rose (Marta Lu Clifford) in the 2011 production of *Salmon Is Everything* at the University of Oregon.

PHOTO: ARIEL OGDEN

I AM KARUK! MY VOICE AS ROSE

Kathleen McCovey

I do not often get an opportunity to speak, or write, from the heart, but that is what I want to do here. I want to tell you how being involved in the development and performance of *Salmon Is Everything* allowed me to speak from the heart in a new way, and to understand that I can help write the history of the Karuk people. I learned that when a story is presented in a way that affects all of the senses—using visual images, body language, and relationships—it can be a very powerful tool for communicating what tribal people on the Klamath River need the world to know and understand.

I had never read for a play before reading a draft of *Salmon Is Everything* aloud to an audience. Theresa asked me to participate in one of the readings of the play-in-progress, to read some of the women's roles. As I read the words, my heart welled up with pride. I could feel my heart get stronger. I was not just reading words, I was speaking many of my own feelings; I was telling people who I really am; I was telling them about the long tie to the land that I and my people have. As I read the lines, my mind's eye envisioned the Klamath River running past my family's village of Ishi Pishi Falls in the canyons of the midriver region.

I remember sitting with my grandmother on a faded gray wooden bench that had been constructed in a circle around the base of a white oak tree. My grandmother and I were looking way down into the canyon of the Klamath River, watching my grandfather dip Salmon out of the River with a traditional Karuk dip net. The bench was full of other women and children who were also watching their men dip for the fall Salmon. My memories of being raised Karuk are of traveling throughout our ancestral territory gathering resources for the winter supply. My memories are of being involved in Karuk ceremonies where we give thanks to the Creator, the Spirit People, the Salmon, and the animals. You see, for the Karuk people, everything has a spirit.

Karuk believe that before we came into the land, the land was inhabited by Spirit People. The Spirit People taught the Karuk how to live upon the land, what to eat, where to live, and how to treat each other, as well as how to interact with other beings, and they taught the people where, when, and how to conduct their ceremonies. When the Spirit People knew that the Karuk knew how to live upon the land, the Spirit People went away. Some of the Spirit People went into the sky, some into the ground, into the water, into the rocks, the trees, the plants, and the animals. As Karuk people, we are never alone in our land because we are always surrounded by Spirit People who help us. We consider ourselves as Karuk people to be related to the Spirit People; they are our brothers and sisters. The Spirit People have formed and still form and influence our relationship to the land and our religious ceremonies. It is the responsibility of the Karuk people to take care of, and live in harmony with, our relations who provide us with the sustenance to live a healthy and happy life along the Klamath River, just as our people have done for thousands of years. I work for the Forest Service as a cultural anthropologist, but as a Karuk person who has a different type of perspective on the landscape, I often find it hard to work for a management agency that does not seem to understand the deep connection that Karuk people have with the land.

In 2004 I was a graduate student in the Environment and Community master's program at Humboldt State University, where I took a class called Art/Culture/Nature from Theresa May. One day after class she told me about *Salmon Is Everything* and asked if I would be willing to be a cultural adviser as the play continued to be developed. This meant that I came to rehearsals and made suggestions, and eventually, I wrote many lines for the character of Rose, a Karuk elder. I remember coming into the theatre for the first time for the reading I mentioned above. I didn't know what to expect and was a little uneasy meeting new people, in a new forum, doing something like acting in front of people—my greatest fear! As the script progressed, we did readings several times in order to get feedback from people. Several readings were at university functions, and my first reading may have been part of the Week of Dialogue on Race, or the Education Summit of that year. The cast was seated onstage in a semicircle; we had music stands in front of us and faced the audience. I was very nervous, and I sat next to Marlon Sherman for a little more security. We reached the middle of the script, the place in the story where the Salmon die and are found downriver in Yurok country during the Jump Dance, one of our most sacred ceremonies. This is the part of the production where the people realize what is happening to the Salmon; the people realize that their relatives are lying along the riverbank suffocating and there is nothing the people can do to help the Salmon People. As I read Rose's lines describing the agony and astonishment that happened on the River, I became overwhelmed with sorrow. My mind split. One half was reading the words; the other was reliving the nightmare. I know the Yurok people well and I know the geographic area where the Salmon died, so I could imagine the scene that I was reading. As I read I became very angry, especially with the government that is charged with managing the water in the Klamath River. Like the play says, before this disaster the Yurok biologists had warned the basin managers about the probable impact of low water on the fish, but their research was ignored. As I read the words aloud, many emotions and images flooded through my mind, and I began to cry. I felt a heavy pain in my heart that comes from the frustration of being misunderstood.

After the reading, a friend of mine from the Hoopa Valley Tribe came down the stairs from the audience and approached me. I looked at him, my eyes still filled with tears, and he looked at me and then he reached out and pulled me to him and gave me a great big bear hug that lasted for a few minutes. We stepped back from each other, looked into each other's eyes, smiled, and he walked away. No words were spoken between us during the whole encounter. We did not have to say anything to each other, for as people of the Klamath and Trinity Rivers, we have a shared history, knowledge, and bond with all the entities of the Rivers that is so deep and so old we need no words. We already know what the other person is thinking and feeling. That hug helped give me the strength to keep working on the play, even though at the same time I was working full-time for the Forest Service, enrolled in graduate school and carrying fifteen units, and driving three hours home to Happy Camp every weekend to take care of my elderly uncle.

As we got closer to the first performance, we established places on the stage with platforms and blocks for the rancher's home and Julie and Rose's home. I stood back and looked at the stage and knew something was missing. I wanted the set to represent what you would find in a Karuk home. I began to bring my Karuk life from my home to the stage. I brought in my gray willow sticks, my baskets, my dress, kishwoof root to burn, and other items that you would find at my house.[22] I also felt I needed to teach the rest of the cast about the items I was bringing, so that they would understand the special knowledge we Karuk and other Klamath River tribes hold about the land. I taught the cast about the basket-making materials, and eventually those teachings became part of the play because it seemed natural for Rose to share her knowledge, just like it is for me.

Karuk science has taught us that certain plants have specific properties that can be utilized throughout the year to improve the quality of life of the people. For example, I showed the cast how to take a gray willow stick, when the sap is running in the spring and fall; the bark strips from the stick with one sweeping stroke of the hand. Little kids just love this trick. In those seasons the sap allows the bark to slip off the willow stick in one solid piece. The trick to getting good sticks is timing, close observation of the growth of the sticks. This was an activity that was easy for us to do right onstage during the scene while everyone was talking, and it's an example of how a visual image—of the family working together with the willow—can mean so much to those watching.

You know, a lot of people think our culture and traditions don't exist anymore. Bringing my regalia and my basket materials to the stage—things from my house, things I handle and use and work with every day—was a kind of proof that we are here! I didn't know if I should bring the ceremonial dress onstage or not, but I wanted people to see, to understand that my grandfather and I hunted the deer; we had those hides tanned; we gathered all of the shells; I gathered the bear grass and wove it. You know, this is what we do! It's part of our life, our ceremonies, our social fabric. The reason I took the dress to rehearsal and then into the performance was because I knew it would be the only chance that some people would have to see anything like it. It's frustrating when surveys ask whether you are white, black, Hispanic, Asian, but almost never Native American. There were so many people on this continent, and that genocide happened in a short amount of time. We cannot just silently stand by and not be counted. Sharing the ceremonial dress that I made with my hands was a way of saying "We're still here!"

My greatest fear was forgetting my lines during performances! I was used to giving presentations on Karuk culture, but in those presentations I didn't have specific lines. There was no other person waiting for me to say the right words in the right order for their cue. Before I went into rehearsal or performance, I would burn kishwoof, our sacred root, and pray for the strength to say the words that I was supposed to say. This might seem funny because the words and parts of the story were my own, but I still had to memorize them! When I would get nervous about going up onstage, I would just think of what the production was about. I would remind myself that I was there to speak for that which has no voice in the world right now, the Salmon People and the Klamath River. My love for my Karuk culture and the world that I live in on the Klamath River is so deep and strong that I will do whatever I have to do to make an impact on people so that they will realize what is happening to the River and our environment. Before a performance, I would calm myself down by remembering who I was and why I was there. And I would look to the other cast members for support. The cast bonded—these people who were strangers are now people I will know for the rest of my life.

Being in the play has given me the strength to stand up, speak the truth from my perspective, and try to undo some of the damage that Euro-American history, so-called Manifest Destiny, has brought on my people and our environment. *Salmon Is Everything* gave me an opportunity to tell some of my story. I felt empowered by the experience of being one of the creators and an actor in this production. Empowerment came from telling other people about what the Klamath River means to Native people like me. The words that we spoke in the performance came from real interviews with real people about the 2002 Salmon kill. Theresa wove feelings, emotions, and events, combining them with staging to allow actors to convey a very ecologically and emotionally complex story to the audience. The audience was interested and very moved by what they were seeing onstage. Perhaps, I thought, people can change the way they think about the world, all from one night at the theatre. I believe this now because I have felt it myself.

One of the things that surprised me about my personal involvement with *Salmon Is Everything* is the intensity of emotion that I felt during almost every scene. In the theatre, a person is free to express herself, and that's not usually the case for Indian people. I have a lot of emotion when I talk about the Salmon kill and its effects on the River and the River communities, and in the theatre that emotion was welcomed. When I found myself crying at rehearsals, Theresa would encourage me and say, "Tears don't have to stop you. Speak through the tears." My voice and my tears help people understand, because then they feel it too. In *Salmon Is Everything* we had a scene where a Salmon symbolizing the thousands of Salmon that had been killed was passed around the stage from one actor to another around a semicircle, until it came to me. I was the last one to hold the Salmon. Every time that the Salmon came out, I would start to cry, because I knew that one Salmon represented thousands of Salmon and other fish and other species that died that year and every year due to the unhealthy condition of the water in the Klamath River. The pain of what had happened and is still happening today to the River and the Salmon is heartbreaking for Klamath River people. I heard some of the audience say that my reaction to the Salmon helped them to understand the depth of pain this event caused us. One of the other women in my graduate program was from the East Coast, and we had become friends over the semester. I did not know she was coming to one of the performances, but afterward she came up to me and said that the performance had made her cry. I was so honored! And I was amazed that a play about my River could affect a person from the East Coast! A person who, before she came to Humboldt State, had no knowledge of the Klamath River and the challenges we face, was moved to tears by watching the play. I thought to myself, no amount of lectures, speeches, or protests could make her cry. Sitting in the audience she had a glimpse into our lives.

Native people can't just pack up and move. The environment, the things in that environment, the native species in that environment, are part of us and our behavior and our management techniques as Native people, which for thousands of years have resulted in the type of ecosystem that we have on the River, with natural Salmon runs of hundreds of thousands. If we're silent we'll be silent witnesses to the devastation of another River system. We have to share the knowledge we have. For example, as a Karuk person who has grown up on the River, I have place-based knowledge about the land that I live on and the species with which I coexist. I am the recipient of thousands of years of knowledge concerning how to survive in the Klamath River watershed. The knowledge that I have about this ecosystem is extensive and cannot be found in forestry classrooms—I know because I have a degree in forestry! I have also been trained as a silviculturist—that is, trained in the art of developing ecosystem management plans for the manipulation of vegetation toward homogeneous conifer stands in public forests. When I have tried to discuss forest management and the manipulation of vegetation to provide resources for Indian communities, those ideas have been rejected as nonsense. Yet that is the way Indian people have always managed their land, by encouraging some plants, or allowing fires to take their course and burn out underbrush, which makes better hunting.

In addition to giving me more self-confidence, being part of *Salmon Is Everything* taught me to recognize a great theatrical opportunity when I see one! I learned that visual scenes may have more impact on people than the spoken word. I took the full opportunity to use what I learned from theatre to get my message through to the shareholders of the company that owns the dams on the Klamath River. This is how it happened.

After the fish kill of 2002, representatives from the Yurok, Karuk, and Hoopa Valley Tribes traveled to Scotland to talk to shareholders of the ScottishPower company, which at the time owned PacifiCorp, the company that manages the dams. The tribes told the stockholders what was happening to the Klamath River, and the Scottish stockholders were appalled; they voted to sell PacifiCorp, and Warren Buffett purchased the company. Since we had been successful in discussing the situation with the Scottish stockholders, in 2008 the tribes went to the Warren Buffett stockholder meeting in Omaha, Nebraska.

Members of our tribe hauled two huge dugout canoes by pickup from California to Nebraska. We set up on the free-speech corner of the Qwest Center (Omaha's convention and conference center) and began to pass out information on the Klamath River issues to shareholders entering the meeting. As our presence became visible, Buffett's shareholders began to learn who we were and why we were there. That reception, however, did not give us the warm understanding we had received in Scotland. The Scottish people are Salmon people too! Perhaps they understood us because they are dependent on fishing. In America, we were not welcomed. Buffett's stockholders spit on us, poked us with umbrellas, told us to go home and get a job, laughed at us, and ridiculed us.

Warren Buffett had a question-and-answer period during his shareholder meetings. The plan was for the tribal representatives at the meeting to sign up for spots at the microphone in order to ask Buffett questions about the Klamath River. We succeeded in loading up all the microphones with tribal members, who asked pointed questions about the Klamath River, the fish kills, and water quality. Buffett could not answer. At noon the shareholder meeting took a lunch break. Before the meeting broke for lunch, Buffett announced that after lunch there would be no more questions about the Klamath River. My turn at the microphone was scheduled for 1 p.m., right after lunch.

When the shareholders gathered together after lunch, the lights were turned down and a spotlight on the microphone came on, and I began walking up for my turn to speak. I was wearing my basket cap and mink hair ties, and I had on my dentillum and abalone necklaces, all symbols of my Northwest coast cultural group. A man dressed in a black suit, a security guard, came toward me on my right side, and I noticed that there was a young man already standing at the microphone where I was to speak. (Had they crossed my name off the list, or grabbed someone to fill my spot? I didn't know.) I continued to walk toward the microphone with every intention to speak, as it was my turn. I could see that the security guard in the black suit was trying to stop me before I got to the microphone, so I began to walk faster. I had a split second to decide how to handle this. I figured the security guard was not going to let me near that microphone. It was then that I remembered my theatre experience and that one picture was worth a thousand words!

I continued to walk, with the man in black in pursuit, until I got into the spotlight. Once I had positioned myself in the spotlight (upstaging the man who was speaking!), I stopped. The security guard stopped in front of me. So there we were, standing in a spotlight in the middle of the dark auditorium, with thirty thousand onlookers. I let the drama play out: a security guard, a big, towering, six-foot, 250-pound man, physically blocking a five-foot-two, 120-pound Karuk woman from speaking at a microphone! I felt like the stage had been set, and I was the actor who had to convey our message from the Salmon with no opportunity to use words. I had to use the resources at hand to get the message across to the people watching. I had positioned myself in the center of the stage for maximum dramatic effect. In that split second, I decided that I was not going to move until my previously allotted time for speaking had been used—by me, not by the young man they no doubt pulled out of the audience to replace me. I looked the security guard directly in the eye and said, "What you are doing to me right now in this spotlight with these people watching will send my message out better than anything I could say if I got to the microphone." And then I said, "Since you will not allow me to speak to the public, I am going to tell you what I wanted to say." With that I began to tell him about the condition of the Klamath River, the fish kill, and the effects of the dams. I kept talking to him until I'd used my three minutes and heard the next speaker being announced. I told the security guard, "My time to speak is up. Thank you for your time." As I turned away from him he looked at me and said, "God bless you." I said "thank you" and turned and walked up the long aisle of the auditorium, aware of thirty thousand people watching me. Bryan Colegrove came down the aisle, took my arm, put it under his, and escorted me out of the building, our heads held high. Other members of our group came up to me and said, "Kathy, that was a great job! We have footage of you being blocked from the speaker by that hulking security guard, and you did not back down, you stood your ground! *That was awesome*!"

Because of the experience I'd had with theatrical acting in the production of *Salmon Is Everything*, I was able to take a situation that seemed to be turned against me and make it work in my favor by knowing how to create a theatrical image that sent a message to thousands of people even though they did not hear a word I said.

It's also important to say here that being involved in the production of *Salmon Is Everything* allowed me to be more sensitive to other people in our watershed. Through characters in the play I felt like I had met farmers, ranchers, commercial fishermen, rafters, and other people who depended on this River. Hearing those perspectives affected me greatly, and I have some sense now of who they are, what their lives are made of, and what they feel in their heart. I am more sensitive to their issues and the circumstances of their lives than I was at the time of the fish kill. We have lots of work to do. Knowing each other's stories, I hope we can do it together.

BECOMING ROSE

Marta Lu Clifford

In 2011 I had the honor of playing Rose in a production of *Salmon Is Everything* at the University of Oregon. The experience changed me in many ways (like all good stories are supposed to do!) and I want to tell you my story of *becoming* Rose.

In Native communities we introduce ourselves by speaking first about the places we come from and who our people are. I am a member of the Confederated Tribes of Grand Ronde, one of the nine federally recognized tribes in the state of Oregon. All nine tribes are made up of peoples from the many Nations that lived in the region we now call Oregon and who were removed from their homeland and placed on reservations to live together. I am Chinook, Cree, Cow Creek Umpqua, and French Canadian from my father; Swiss and German from my mother. I am proud to be Grand Ronde and honored to be called an Elder in my tribal community. I was born in Oregon into a large loving family, the seventh of nine children. I had a fun, carefree childhood living in rural Douglas County, where "timber was king." But when my father died in1960, my mother packed us up and moved us to Springfield, Oregon, to be close to her mother, our grandmother. Springfield is still my home, and I love walking this land and exploring our beautiful state. I have a goal to see how many waterfalls I can see in a year! I'm a mother to a wonderful daughter who has always been my inspiration. She flew all the way from Washington, DC, to see me perform in *Salmon Is Everything.*

I heard about the play by chance. One spring day I stopped in at the Grand Ronde office to drop off some homemade jam for my niece, who worked there. She told me she had heard about a play that was going to be done at the university about the fish kill on the Klamath River, and that it had some Native characters. (The fact that I had heard about it in my own tribal office meant that someone had done their outreach to invite us in and ask for our consultation and participation.) The next day my sister also said, "Marta, did you hear, someone at the UO is doing a play about the Salmon? They are looking for someone to play the part of an elder. You should check it out." My sister remembered the acting I had done long ago and how much I loved it. I decided I would be brave and go see. I had to stay brave, and determined, as I parked near the university, walked across the street, through two giant metal gates, and gazed up at the imposing Robinson Theatre. I had to quiet the voices in my head as I walked up its long cascade of stairs and went inside. Even if I didn't get the part, I told myself, I need to see what this Salmon play is all about! As I opened the door I could hear voices, and I followed them until I found a large group of people walking around the stage, all talking and holding scripts. I didn't know what to do next: Who's in charge? I saw a kind looking woman with dark curly hair. I don't know if she is the director but she looks like she will be easy to talk to, I thought to myself. I had chosen the right person to talk to. Theresa May greeted me with a smile and a warm handshake. I think she could tell I was a little nervous about being there. "I heard you were looking for an elder to be in a play," I said. We chatted a bit about the rehearsal schedule and what was involved. And then she handed me a script, saying that the cast was about to start a first read-through of the play, would I join them? I said, Yes! And then Theresa introduced me to the circle of actors saying, "I think we may have found our Rose." I guess I got the part! I thought. What I didn't know then, and what I still tell people when I talk about my experience being in *Salmon Is Everything*: the moment when Theresa handed me my script was the beginning of becoming Rose, and it would change my life in many positive ways I could not have predicted.

Theatre does that. On stage or in the audience, theatre can transform people. Theatre can empower and move people to activism; it can affect us emotionally, creating compassion and a sense of connection, and I believe it can help people and communities heal. In this play we had a responsibility to tell the story of the people on the Klamath River and the Salmon they depend on for their physical, spiritual, and cultural existence. But first, I had to learn my lines! Becoming Rose involved many hours of dedicated practice, and there were many times that I thought, "I will not be able to memorize all these words I am supposed to speak!" But after a few weeks something changed for me. This group of seventeen people who didn't know each other had transformed into what I started to call our "Salmon family." As we learned our lines and remembered where to stand or sit; as we learned our dances and practiced the Lamentation scene; as we talked about our characters' relationships to other characters in the play, the whole cast became dedicated to each other, like a family. We understood and felt the importance of the story we were telling, right down to our bones. Once we had faith in the purpose of the production, learning lines was so much easier! Don't get me wrong, theater is a huge amount of work, but became a labor of love—like the Salmon swimming upstream.

Rehearsals took patience as we figured out how we wanted to tell this story. We wanted the audience to feel connected to what was happening on stage. We wanted to invite the people who would fill those two hundred empty seats into our world, the world of the Salmon. The set designer, Dan Carlgren, worked with Gordon Bettles, the steward of the Many Nation's Longhouse on campus, to create a stage that looked like the inside of a longhouse. It felt warm and inviting, and with just a few chairs and props, the actors could transform a pool of light into the home of each of the three family groups in the play.

As we got closer to the day we would have an audience in those two hundred seats, Theresa suggested that we start the play with actors sitting in the audience: characters would then emerge *from the audience*, and one by one, walk down and onto the stage. I wasn't sure how this would work. In every play I'd ever seen the actors and the audience are separate. But "let's try it," Theresa said. I will admit on opening night, when I took my seat in the audience with the actress playing Little Mary by my side, I was nervous. What are people thinking of me? They don't know I am part of the cast! What if I see someone I know and they come up and talk to me? Do they just see a Native woman who has brought her granddaughter to see this play about her people? As I sat with the audience waiting for the lights to go down I kept thinking, am I myself, or am I Rose, the Karuk Elder? It was like an out-of-body experience—I was sitting there as Rose but watching people taking their seats, commenting on the beautiful set on stage, and listening to the music. I was also thinking, wow, not many Native people here! I hope the audience listens to our story and understand the importance of our message about the Salmon. But as soon as the lights go down and the water and landscape are projected on the stage, and the Salmon Dancer comes from the back of the theatre, dancing down the stairs, as soon as she gestures to me, as if to say, "I recognize you, Rose. Let's tell this story together for the people that live on the Klamath River. Let's tell the story of our Salmon family that need our help"—at that moment, I stand and say without any fear, "I am Karuk!" And then I am Rose. I can feel the power of the words, and the pride. "I am Karuk!" For the next two hours, I am Rose, the Karuk Elder, who is a mother, grandmother, basket weaver, artist, storyteller, and the keeper of the family culture and traditions. I had some big shoes to fill! Every night of the performance, when I would change into the garments that would transform me into Rose and put on my makeup, which included the traditional chin marks worn by the Karuk Elders, that same sense of pride carried me and filled me like a power that I felt deep inside. I would speak for the Salmon and the people who live along the Klamath River. I would let the story take me, and I would become Rose! It was wonderful! Every night, from those first words until the end of the play, I felt like I was telling real stories about real people, and that I was speaking for someone very special—which I was.

It was not until two years later, when the first edition of this book was published, that I read Kathleen McCovey's story about her own experience helping to develop the play, writing the words of Rose, sharing her traditional knowledge, and, like me, working up the courage to be on stage. In a way, I met Kathleen through her words. When

I read her chapter, I was amazed that she seemed to be describing *my* experience in the performance, too:

> We reached the middle of the script, the place in the story where the Salmon die and are found downriver in Yurok country during the Jump Dance, one of our most sacred ceremonies. This is the part of the production where the people realize what is happening to the Salmon; the people realize that their relatives are lying along the riverbank suffocating and there is nothing the people can do to help the Salmon People. As I read Rose's lines describing the agony and astonishment that happened on the River, I became overwhelmed with sorrow. My mind split. One half was reading the words; the other was reliving the nightmare (97).

Now I am in awe at Kathleen's courage and the strong Karuk woman's voice she gave to Rose and to the Salmon People. Thank you, Kathleen, for giving a voice to Rose—that allowed me to give a voice to Rose in Eugene, Oregon! Perhaps this is the power of theater—this feeling that she was speaking through me, and we were both speaking together for others, for the Salmon. So many of her words tore at my heart and touched me deeply that they randomly pop into my head still, and I will say them to myself, or out loud if no one is around: "Sacred is the stories that we were given from our Elders, who learned them from their Elders. Sacred is our prayer medicine that carries my prayers, hopes, and dreams up to Creator every night. Our ceremonies are sacred and bring life, repairing bad feelings or wrong actions." Even now, as I write her words, I re-live being on the Robinson stage where I spoke Kathleen's words and told her story and felt her pain. Kathleen shared her story through the fictional role of Rose, and through those words, I am moved and changed in becoming Rose. It is difficult to describe the power of this connection, but this is the power of stories, the power of theater.

Becoming Rose has made me more aware of our larger Native community throughout Oregon, connected me to a new family at the University of Oregon, and renewed my love of theatre. It has put me on a journey with new and exciting experiences around every corner. I keep in touch with many of the students who were in the play: I call them my "Salmon children." After the production of *Salmon Is Everything,* I took Theresa's course in Native theatre and fell in love with the many plays written by contemporary Native and First Nations playwrights.[23] After that first class, I have served as an Elder in Residence in the course, working with Native and non-Native students, helping them to appreciate the diverse voices of our Native playwrights and to understand the cultural context and knowledge in the plays. I have gotten to know UO's Native faculty, and have been a speaker in their classes. As my friendship and collaboration with Theresa has grown, we have started presenting public readings of Native plays to the community. I love being a part of the growing awareness of the potential for Native theatre in our community. Theatre can create change for others, as becoming Rose in *Salmon Is Everything* has for me, because it touches mind, heart, body, and soul.

I have always been aware of our responsibility to care for the Earth, but becoming Rose also inspired me to be more active in preserving our traditional ecological knowledge and ways of caring for the earth and water. Salmon are sacred to the Native people of Oregon, one of the "first foods" of Oregon's first people. They are a "keystone species," which means that the ecological systems of our land, including the health of the people, are linked to the health of the Salmon. When Rose says in the play, "we need to once again take care of the Salmon physically and spiritually. This is the time for their survival and ours," she is talking about a sacred trust, and the exercise of traditional knowledge of Indigenous People everywhere.

It was an honor to play Rose, and to be welcomed into our Native theatre community. I look forward to sharing more stories!

THE EDUCATION OF AN ARTIST

Theresa May

When I went to my colleague Suzanne Burcell with the idea to develop a community-based play that told the story of the 2002 fish kill from a Native perspective, I did not have all my ducks lined up. That turned out to be a good thing. In the chapter that follows I relate moments in my own process of transformation as a non-Native/settler artist and academic, working in collaboration with Native and non-Native students, faculty, staff, and community members. Every step of the way—from gathering a group of collaborators to weaving the play and directing it onstage—challenged me in immediate and sometimes uncomfortable ways.

New to the watershed, I learned on the fly, meeting people and problems as we do in life—by being thrust into the middle of things, learning about the past as we navigate the present. I had seen some of the pain and suffering caused by the ecological and political imbalances on the Klamath River, and I believed theatre could be a useful tool for social change and community healing. But good intentions did not mean that the project was immune to history. In community-based projects such as this one, history complicates the work and the relationships on which it depends in constant and sometimes subtle ways. From the first contact of euroamerican settlers with Indigenous residents, to the most recent cross talk at Klamath watershed conferences, history is alive. Native people are understandably wary of the social, political, educational, and economic institutions that have been part of a long colonial history of appropriation. As a euroamerican settler descendant and an employee of an institution with roots in colonialism, I represented that history. This project, I quickly learned, would repeatedly ask me to own that history and check my privilege.

We held the first community meeting about the Klamath Theatre Project on campus one evening, and I brought snacks and sodas. For the first hour, no one came. Trying to hide my disappointment, I made small talk with Sue Burcell and our colleague Phil Zastrow, a Hupa tribal member. Finally, a few people trickled in, including Marlon Sherman, a Lakota Sioux poet and professor of Native studies who would later become an important adviser on the project, and members of the Native community including Native artists and representatives from Indian Health Services, as well as a number of Native and non-Native students. After introductions, I began to present my idea. A few sentences into my notes, one of the elders stopped me and said, "Who are you?! What are we doing here listening to you? What's all this talk about telling an Indian story when we're sitting in a classroom of a racist institution?" I was brought up short. After what seemed like an eternal silence, Sue, in her characteristically calming way, spoke about the possibility that this artist (me) was willing to offer her skills to work with the Native students and community to tell their story in a new way, a way that might help express Native perspectives about the salmon. She explained that as far as she could tell, I had come "with a good heart" to talk with her and ask for collaboration—partnership that she was willing to give and see where it led. The moment passed and my embarrassment subsided, although I never did get back to my notes! Instead, I listened and took notes.

Elders and students spoke for another two hours about the recent fish kill, the need for Native voices to be heard, the importance of community involvement, and their fears of institutional control. Near the end of the evening Sue asked if there was consensus that the project should move forward with community participation. Yes, the group agreed, as long as the university would not own people's stories, and as long as Native people were involved and consulted throughout the process so that the end product reflected the values of the Native community.

FIRST GATHERINGS

My collaborators included Native faculty and staff, community members, and a core group of Native and non-Native students, some of whom were able to participate in the project for course credit. The structure of our work together was simple and fluid. We met twice a week in the late afternoon and evening after work and classes. I brought snacks to sustain our energy and to help forge the bonds of community and exchange that we would need going forward. We shared our research and discussed the issues; we completed writing exercises and then read them aloud. We interviewed individuals and groups in the Klamath watershed. Native collaborators interviewed family and extended family members; non-Native collaborators interviewed commercial fishermen, white-water rafters, environmentalists, and agency personnel. We went on field trips to the mouth of the Klamath River, and to ceremonial sites.

The students contributed to the shape of the play not only through their research and writing but also through the many ways they shared their lives with me. Reflective writing (free writing) allowed each individual to sort out her or his own thoughts and feelings about many aspects of the fish kill, and, as it turned out, what it meant to identify as a Native young person at this moment in history. Many of the scenes, ideas, and characters that eventually became part of the play arose not so much from the research we did, or even the interviews, but from the stories that emerged spontaneously out of our day-to-day relationships as a collaborative group. Below, I trace parts of the play back to those seed moments.

Several of the Native students were parents and they brought their children along to our meetings. Our discussions were often punctuated by the voices and needs of toddlers, and by phone calls with extended family about rides, meals, and child care. At first I worried that we would never get anything done under these circumstances, but I soon realized that few people multitask better than a young Native woman who is a single parent and a student. I also realized that if a play or performance were to grow out of our collaboration, it needed to do so in the midst of, and not in spite of, family. These little ones would inherit stewardship of the salmon; their presence was the living flesh of our reason for coming together. From the beginning, children were part of every working session and rehearsal.

At our first meeting I asked the group members to talk about their personal connection to the salmon, the river, and the recent fish kill. Through our conversations and their responses, the group began teaching me not only about the significance of salmon in Native culture but also about the complicated politics among the tribes of the watershed. As they shared stories and knowledge with me and with one another, I began to understand the salmon in new ways. While her three-year-old watched a Disney DVD on the computer, Heather Hostler told us, "Salmon is one of the first foods we feed our children. The mom takes some salmon and chews it a little and then gives it to her baby." "First food" had a double meaning in Heather's comment. The term also refers to the traditional and indigenous foods that Native peoples depended on prior to foods introduced by settlers. For northern California and Oregon tribal peoples, first foods include salmon, sturgeon, trout, eel, deer, elk, acorns, huckleberries, salal berries, camas root, and many other native plants and animals. Salmon is at the center of the circle of first foods because the health of the watershed as a whole is connected to the health of salmon populations.[24] Ultimately, the play would be infused with the kinship of family—family that included the salmon.

"INDIAN TIME"

Our meetings never began on time. Often, one or more of the group came late, and absences were frequent. At first I thought this indicated a lack of commitment to the project, and I grumbled to myself. Slowly, however, I began to understand the larger context of my collaborators' lives. Native young people live "in two worlds," as my Klamath colleague Gordon Bettles often points out.[25] The project was merely one aspect of lives in which family obligations, cultural traditions and geography, as well as academic and economic pressures, were intertwined. Sometimes we would not hear from a member of the group for several weeks. "Oh, she had to go up to Crescent City to help her mom," one of the others would tell me. When I suggested that she might have called, the others reminded me, "There's no cell phone service up there." They kept one another's privacy regarding extended family obligations and did not tell me the details. In addition to being young mothers in school, some of these women were coping with the long-term effects of colonization within their families and communities—poverty, drug and alcohol addiction, as well as health impacts that were the result of the loss of traditional foods. For many, being in school at all was a personal achievement; meeting regularly with a professor to work on a play was a near miracle. As I learned more about my collaborators' multifaceted roles as mothers, daughters, granddaughters, students, wives, and partners, I grew to admire them and trust their judgment. They came when they came, and things got done when they got done. As I became accustomed to the rhythms of our work together, *my* faith in the project grew.

Working through these frustrations opened up my understanding about my own Western concepts of time itself. One afternoon in those first few weeks, Phil Zastrow asked how the project was going. I told him about the lateness and absences, hoping for some advice from a Native colleague. "Oh, you're on Indian time!" he laughed. I'd heard the expression on campus and had bristled at what I thought was one more pejorative figure of speech that marginalized Native people. But now it was my Hupa colleague speaking, and something I needed to learn if the project was to succeed. From an indigenous philosophical perspective, time is fluid, responding to seasons, honoring relationships and urgencies as they arise in everyday life. In contrast, the idea of regulated, incremental, and regimented minutes, hours, days, weeks, and so on is only *one* way of understanding and organizing time. This "white time" is also a culturally constructed sensibility meant to enforce sacrosanct behaviors including punctuality and meeting external deadlines. This so-called "good time management" runs the risk of devaluing the very aspects of lived experience that were at the heart of our project: family, relationship, and being part of the larger cycles of the world around us. I began to recognize that the privileging of white time constitutes an institutional bias that gives disproportional advantage to one set of cultural values while it disadvantages another. Furthermore, modes of working that are lauded in the academy, such as planning strategies, predicting results, tracking trajectories, and noting "benchmark" accomplishments may be primarily performative behaviors meant to communicate authority and maintain control. In this way, certain normative expectations around time may increase experiences of exclusion, while they disguise and perpetuate institutional racism.

I began to notice the way white time tended to marginalize highly effective ways of working. Native people of the Klamath River have been well organized for thousands of years around the seasonal migration of the salmon, around the readiness of huckleberries and acorns for harvest, and around myriad other subtle cycles of change in the land and its biotic communities.[26] Likewise, other endeavors including social gatherings, family functions, ceremonies, education, and creative projects all move to a time that is indigenous to that community, place, and project. Our work together—the research, writing, and rehearsals—would also have a time of its own. If I became intent on bringing something to fruition merely because I faced the end of a grant cycle or academic term, I would be working in the wrong way and would fail my collaborators and the salmon.

The idea that concepts of time are cultural and spiritual as well as practical, and that tasks such as food gathering and creative work can be organized differently, would find its way into scene 14 of the play in the words of the character of Rachel, who criticizes Kate for living only by "rational time." Respecting my collaborators' intuitive sense of time would also save me enormous frustration when the project moved into rehearsal and production two years later. As we came closer to our first performance, a sense of urgency quickened in the group. Everyone came early, stayed late, and worked with patience and willingness to solve problems quickly and efficiently.

THE INTERVIEWS

In conceiving the project, I had anticipated conducting interviews with community members and using this material as the basis for writing the play. But when the time came to begin interviews, I was unable to muster the sense of authority that I imagined other artists had when working with communities.[27] Suddenly, work that I had admired, such as the issue-engaged plays of Anna Deavere Smith, Moisés Kaufman, or Ping Chong, became ethically suspect.[28] What right do I have to gather the emotional artifacts of a collective trauma? My doubts seemed to call into question the very project of community-based theatre. As a non-Native person, how could I ask students to conduct interviews with tribal community members about the fish kill? I am neither a relative nor someone directly impacted by the fish kill. What differentiates me from artists who seem to appropriate the suffering of others as raw materials for art making when they are not members of that community? Or worse, how am I different from those who searched for gold in the mountains and rivers of the Klamath watershed? What *is* my relationship to the fish kill and the river? This confrontation with my own investment in, and connection to, the issues and the play would later take shape in a scene between the characters of Kate and Julie. At the moment, however, my status as outsider loomed large in my mind, and I found myself paralyzed.

I shared my doubts with my collaborators. Would it be a good idea, I asked, to talk to people upriver, to talk to your families and people in the tribal communities about what happened? If we did, how should we go about it? In retrospect, I cannot stress strongly enough that as artists we must be sure of one thing: we do not always know how to do it. We must turn to our collaborators—the community we serve and of which we are a part—and ask. Doing so precipitates knowledge sharing, which is, after all, a central purpose of community-based work. The very act of turning to someone across the divide of culture, age, ability, or educational difference to ask, "What would you do? What do you think?" is to say, in effect, "Teach me." This knowledge sharing not only affirms community, it forges community.

"We can do interviews if we do them with respect," the Native students said. "It must be us doing the interviews, not you. I can ask my grandmother questions, or my uncle, and that makes sense, that's not disrespectful." They reaffirmed what Dudley Cocke of the Roadside Theatre has claimed, that this kind of theatre work grows out of long-term and ongoing relationships. It is not a swoop in, swoop out affair.[29] I suggested that each of us make a personal list of people *in our own lives* that we might interview about the fish kill. A non-Native student looked at me quizzically and complained she would have no one to interview. I realized she felt excluded. I asked her to think of people who might have been affected by the fish kill with whom she had a relationship or who were her peers; for example, other students, teachers, or someone from a local business. Then a light bulb went on. Her eyes beamed as she remembered taking a white-water rafting trip on the Trinity River the previous summer. "I can interview the white-water guide!" In that moment, the project became personal to her. No longer merely an intellectual or artistic exercise, it was an investigation into her own life and how she was connected to the river and the fish. Similarly, I made a list for myself that included colleagues at the university, health care workers, people from the environmental community, and government agency personnel. My self-doubt had helped decenter my status as project director, faculty, and artist; those doubts, honestly shared, gave rise to the very structure of our work together, a structure that had both integrity and efficacy.

Next, we discussed how we might compose interview questions that were appropriate. Questions to elders needed to be quite general, the Native students told me, so that the person being interviewed could take the conversation in whatever direction felt right. If an elder answered a question about the fish kill by talking about a childhood memory or telling a story, that needed to be respected.

"Elders don't always answer the question that you ask!" they warned. "They might think something else is more important." The Native students intuitively understood that a project like this must respond and adapt fluidly and generously to the unpredictable contributions of the community.

Even though the group had talked about who should interview whom, the process was not without risk. Some of the Native students also had concerns that the topic might be too painful for their relatives and friends to discuss. "My grandmother might not want to talk about it. She was there and I remember her crying, and I don't want to make her remember it." Heather explained that some of the elders felt that the fish kill was the Native people's fault. "Our people used to do the First Salmon Ceremony, and some of the elders think we should be doing it now, but there are not very many people who remember how it's done," she told us.[30] Many in the group returned to our next gathering surprised that their families and friends were willing and often eager to talk about the fish kill and its cultural, legal, and ecological ramifications. "My grandmother got going and then she wouldn't stop!" one student exclaimed. Sharing my own fears and hesitations with my collaborators had the unexpected effect of bolstering their own courage to talk to their families. Since interviews were conducted by individuals who already had a relationship with the person being interviewed, student and community trust in the project grew.

FREE WRITING

Each week I gave a prompting question that was followed by ten to fifteen minutes of reflective writing. The immediacy of the act of writing allowed group members to express personal knowledge about the issues and find their voices. Likewise, reading these writings aloud to one another built confidence and authority in these young writers, clarified their feelings, and personalized their stake in the river. The students produced a rich array of poetry and prose that included personal memories, imagined dialogue with family and community, philosophical musings, and fragments of stories handed down through oral tradition. For example, a Yurok woman wrote a story about camping near the smoking pits to protect the fresh-caught salmon from the bears, and a Karuk woman wrote about sleeping outdoors with her cousins at ceremony time. These and other impromptu essays became part of scene 2.

Our meetings were a time for sharing stories and knowledge (the products of their research and writing), but also a time for sharing the challenges and frustrations of their everyday lives. It's hard to balance being a student and a mother, getting homework done, finding child care, getting to class, having two jobs, and then, "sometimes we have to deal with extended family members in crisis," they told me. "Yeah, there are weeks when there isn't enough money to put gas in the car to drive up to Orleans to help a relative, and then have enough left over for food and school supplies!" Then someone observed, "We're just like the salmon, trying to swim upstream in a river that doesn't have enough water in it!" I asked them to take a few minutes and write about these frustrating experiences. Lauren Taylor wrote a story about picking up two tourists who had been fishing on the Klamath. Her story paints a textured picture of a young Yurok woman's day-to-day life on California's north coast, and it became part of scene 7. As our work continued, these pieces of creative nonfiction, which communicated so much cultural knowledge, became the real heart of the work.

As I began to know each of my collaborators as complex individuals, I knew that the play would ultimately be populated by young characters. I imagined that the central character of the play could be a composite of these bright young Native women. In the play, the character of Julie moves between worlds—from her grandmother's traditional home space to the science lab and fieldwork. Like several of my young collaborators, the character of Julie attends meetings with a baby in her arms. She struggles to make ends meet, maintain her relationship, and care for her elders and child. All this is part of what drives her activism on behalf of the salmon.

THE MOUTH OF THE KLAMATH

I suggested we take a field trip to the mouth of the Klamath River—the site of the 2002 fish kill. The river meets the Pacific about an hour's drive north of Arcata on Highway 101, near the small town of Klamath, where a bridge with two golden bears on either side spans the wide girth of the river.[31] Hand-painted signs along the roadway advertise fresh-caught and smoked salmon. Jet boat companies, a couple of bars, and a stop-and-go store that caters to sportfishermen are, in addition to the tribal casino, the only businesses. On the right, about a quarter mile north of the bridge, is the Yurok Tribal Headquarters—a large, beautiful building made of cedar and stone, flanked by several dozen mobile homes, a gas station, and another stop-and-go. The closest supermarket, drugstore, and hardware store are another sixty miles north in Crescent City.

On the ocean side, Requa Road leads from the highway out to a gravel parking area with a cement boat ramp at the river's edge. As we piled out of cars, a Yurok student said, "This is where everyone parks their campers and puts their boat in to fish." Pointing south across the river to several small cedar buildings on the far shore, she added, "That's where we have the Brush Dance."[32] I took out my binoculars and looked at the three ceremonial houses sitting quiet and silent across the water. "Hey," someone said, pointing to a group of boys out toward the ocean at the edge of a sandbar where the water from the river and ocean swirled together and made a deep pool in the sand. "What's *he* doing out here?!" "Who is it?" the others chimed. "Can I have your binoculars?" another asked me. In a moment they were all giggles, passing my binoculars between them, looking at a group of four or five young men around a large pool of water. "What are they doing?" I asked. "Eeling!" "They're fishing for eels. Lamprey eel is our other main food we take from the river." "You have a long stick with a hooked part on the end and you dip it in and hook the eel." Lauren described an eel hook that she'd seen once, made from elk antler. "Traditionally, it's men and boys' work, but I really want to learn to do it." Both Lauren's and Heather's daughters were with us that day, and they hung on their mothers' arms and cried out, "I want to do it, I want to do it!" This is one of many sweet moments that I marked in memory as a potential part of the play.

We drove back on Requa Road and took the road to the right of an old inn founded in the 1920s for tourists and sportfishermen. At the top of the ridge, where a small national park viewpoint overlooked the mouth of the Klamath, other sightseers were searching the horizon for whales. An illustrated interpretive display described the "first peoples" of the Klamath. "I remember when they made this. They came and wanted old photos from the elders," one of the group said, and another pointed to a black-and-white photo in the display. "Hey, I know that guy! He lives up at Orleans," she told us. I was struck for a moment that the living grandchildren of those "first peoples" pictured in the park interpretive display were standing next to me, lively and chattering, concerned with the boys down at the eeling pool, and asking when we were going to have lunch. I wondered what it felt like to have people you know "interpreted" for tourists, as

Shifting sandbars form at the mouth of the Klamath River. Photo: U.S. Army Corps of Engineers.

if they were historic relics. Perhaps the display should be amended: "P.S. We're still here!"

From high up we looked down on two sandbars—one short, one long—that divide the river's mouth from the welcoming sea. I think it was Lauren who told us a story that she'd heard from a relative: two sisters sit on either side of the mouth of the river; one has her legs outstretched and one keeps her legs tucked under. When they get tired of sitting in their position, the sisters switch. The sister with legs tucked gets to stretch her legs out while the other tucks. These sisters are the guardians of the mouth of the river. The story explains why sometimes, during a winter of heavy storms, the sandbars dramatically change shape. The place where the water enters the sea can move hundreds of yards up or down the beach as a result of winter storms. When this happens, people say that the sisters have changed their pose.

The place we would have lunch and spend most of the afternoon was back across the bridge to the south bank, where the road stopped at the Yurok ceremonial grounds. We grabbed journals, jackets, and food and walked along a path under tall cedar and alder trees, past the three ceremonial houses. The Native women described their uses: one for the men, one for the women, and one for the regalia. Men and women dressed and danced separately, each charged with certain prayers. The dance pit was dug into the earth about twelve feet deep and about twenty feet square, with a circle of stones in the middle for the fire. Benches around the pit allowed people who were not dancing to watch and be included in the prayers.

Meanwhile, someone noticed white spray-painted graffiti on the door of one of the houses. One of the Native students said in disgust, "Probably some [insert your own expletive] white kids did that!" This is the first moment—in a process that would include many such moments—I recall having a visceral (vs. intellectual) sense of my own white settler ancestry. As I stood on ceremonial ground with young people for whom that ground was home, I thought about how such moments were probably commonplace for them. The experience marked a learning for me, and one that I think must be understood by anyone who wants to work with young people from communities that have been historically marginalized or devalued: to be a person of settler descent in a position of authority, engaged in a project such as this, requires a willingness to be present to anger and generational grief. Were my collaborators so comfortable with me that they could speak candidly? Were they testing me? Or were they as embarrassed by the graffiti as I was? I knew their anger was both at me and not at me. It was part of my job to know that I was not the target, but at the same time to comprehend the legitimacy of their anger. Their anger was not about me personally, yet it was about my history and the privilege I had inherited, and it had come to rest on my shoulders for the moment. The sensation was never pleasant, but it was an important part of learning how the past always walks with us. In such moments I felt it was my turn to catch the ball that history had thrown. The more I understood the dynamics of generational grief, the more I was willing, and honored, to catch it. To allow the anger to be expressed, to be present to it, hear it, and acknowledge its legitimacy was part of what I had signed on to do.

FIRST CONCERT READING

By the end of winter term, the group members were anxious to know how the material we had collected and written would become a play, and I suggested that it might be time to hear some of it read aloud. A concert reading, I told them, would allow us to listen for the truth of emerging characters, language, and imagery, and after the reading we would invite the community to give us feedback and suggestions. Throughout the development of *Salmon Is Everything* we were committed to ongoing dialogue with community members. As Jan Cohen-Cruz has written, this "reciprocity" is one of the principles of community-based theatre and implies a kind of input loop from the community back into the creative process of the artists.[33] The conversations that took place after the many public readings of the play-in-progress contributed immensely, often in ways we did not expect, to the development of the play. In this way the community helped shape the play, but perhaps more importantly, the existence of the play—even in its rudimentary form—constituted a forum where communicative democracy was taking place.

In preparation for the reading, I selected and stitched together some of the paragraphs, poems, interviews, and news items that we had collected or written. Weaving in my own writing as needed, I combined the material into loose composite characters: a woman elder, a young Native woman studying wildlife biology, a young subsistence fisherman, and a collection of secondary characters who formed their community. But when I proposed they read their work aloud, the Native women in the group wanted nothing to do with performing. "What, *act*? Are you kidding?!" Flummoxed at first, I wondered if listening might be even better. Perhaps then they would hear the dramatic potential in their writing. I recruited some willing Native faculty and staff along with a few theatre students and community actors as readers, secretly hoping the reading might inspire my young Native collaborators to *want* to perform the next time.

The reading attracted a diverse audience from the tribal community, students, faculty, and local environmentalists. My collaborators took charge of welcoming the audience and we brought food to share during the discussion that followed. I was happy to see so many Native people attend this first reading; and I was nervous. I explained to the audience that we wanted to share what we had written in order to hear their thoughts about the direction the play was taking, and so that they (the community) could help us (the writers) hear what stories were beginning to emerge, and what stories and voices were still missing. I stressed that this was a work-in-progress, a living document that would be shaped by what they offered in the discussion that followed. I also asked the audience to pay special attention to the images that came to mind as they were listening, explaining that the feedback from their minds' eyes would help us envision the play. The reading lasted about one hour, and the discussion lasted two more hours as community members expressed their response to the play and shared their communal grief and anger around the fish kill.

My colleague and playwright Margaret Kelso helped facilitate the discussion, and my collaborators sat onstage with her so they could answer questions and also be recognized for their work. I'd asked Jean O'Hara, a friend and former graduate student, to help me take notes on the community response. We sat off to the side of the theatre, scribbling fast and furious as the conversation unfolded. Margaret first asked, "What images, scenes, or words were most powerful or meaningful?" Then, "What rang false or seemed incomplete?" And finally, "What or who still needs to be part of this story?" Consensus indicated that the play-in-progress reflected a Native point of view, consistent with the original intent of the project. The audience affirmed that these were the voices that were not getting press in the Klamath Basin, even as the plight of the ranchers and farmers had become national news. The community members came alive with their own memories and experiences, sharing with us a bounty of new information, feelings, and perspectives. Elders from the tribal communities responded to the reading by telling more stories. A woman said, "Yes, yes, it was just that way. It was at the Brush Dance out at Requa and we were fixing food and we hear someone calling from the river and my little son is walking up the bank with a dead fish in his arms! That's how we discovered what had happened. Then we all went down to the river and there they were, dead salmon floating and laying on the shore." Another woman said, "The smell! You have to include the smell of the fish, the smell of death!" Someone else remembered that schools were closed due to the smell. They gave us many suggestions: "I hear the sound of Brush Dancing," and another chimed in, "We need images of the river, people fishing and dancing!"

Then one elder opened a door that shifted the conversation. "We need the farmers' stories too! We need to invite them down for a salmon dinner after the play!" Others echoed agreement. "We need to have a big salmon bake and invite the farmers and ranchers from upriver to come down and share food at our table. Maybe then they'd understand." "Yes," another said, "but we also need to go up there and eat—what *do* they eat?" "Beef and potatoes!" Everyone laughed, but the air was also filled with the spirit of generosity that arises organically from the experience of being heard. Choctaw playwright LeAnne Howe writes about the power of Native stories not only to communicate ideas, but more importantly to create new worlds, new realities. "Native stories are power. They create people. They author tribes."[34] As stories poured forth from the community, so did a creative force that would change the course of the project. "We need to sit down and have a meal with them and learn what's important to them," one of the elders continued, turning the conversation in a direction I had not anticipated. "Farmers have to be in this play too," continued the cacophony of agreement. "The play needs to keep the Indian focus, because that's its purpose, to tell the story from our perspective, but it's not *only* our perspective. We have to tell the larger story. They have families, right? If we could hear each other's stories, then maybe things could change because people would understand." If I had suggested that the play include the perspective of farmers and ranchers, the idea would have seemed artificial. But the elders charged us to include the voices of the Upper Klamath community (including the Klamath Tribes), not only as background material but as possible elements of the play. Our next draft included voices from a wider watershed.

SPEAKING FROM THE HEART

One morning I received a call from Denice Helwig, who worked in the president's office of Humboldt State University. She invited me to join her at a Klamath watershed stakeholder gathering to be held in Somes Bar, near the confluence of the Klamath and Salmon Rivers. I did not know then that I would be attending a gathering that would mark a shift in watershed politics. I went with an interest in finding out more about the history and politics of the river, especially about the Upper Klamath Basin—a place that seemed remote to those of us in Humboldt and Del Norte Counties, but that clearly impacted the quality of life in tribal communities on the Lower Klamath. At this meeting I became acquainted with the people behind many of the complex conflicts in the watershed. I listened to personal stories and viewpoints of farmers, ranchers, commercial fishers, and government officials from county, state, and federal agencies related to wildlife, water, and land management. When I told them about the play, many were enthusiastic about the idea of theatre as a forum for building understanding across the two cultures.

The gathering at Somes Bar marked a new approach to negotiation in the Klamath watershed and was the first in a series of stakeholder meetings led by conflict resolution consultants Bob Chadwick and Terry Morton of Consensus Associates.[35] Between 2001 and 2003, the Klamath Basin Ecosystem Foundation, under the direction of Mike Connelly, had organized several watershed conferences, hoping to mitigate polarization. But Connelly and others had become increasingly frustrated by the adversarial post–fish kill politics. The policy-justifying presentations of conference forums seemed to entrench opposing sides of the debate rather than change hearts and minds or mediate differences. Connelly and others were ready for a new approach to watershed dialogue and invited Chadwick, a longtime basin resident and professional mediator, to step in with a consensus-building approach.

I attended three of the Chadwick sessions—in Somes Bar in the Mid-Klamath, at Yurok Headquarters in Klamath, and at Tule Lake in the Upper Klamath Basin. Chadwick sessions were also held in Scott Valley and Chiloquin. These gatherings were designed to help water users get past divisiveness and to find common ground and common cause. In his book *River of Renewal*, Stephen Most describes the Chadwick sessions in some detail. My own memories are still vivid.

Denice and I took empty chairs in a circle of about twenty-five people seated under the canopy of several large oak trees. It was a hot day in the Klamath high country, and the shade was a welcome respite after the two-hour drive from Arcata on a winding road that had been carved into the rugged mountains on one side and plummeted down to the Klamath River on the other. Acorns crunched underfoot as one person and then another silently entered the circle and sat down. The pre-presentation networking chatter typical of conferences was markedly absent. Some people exchanged quiet greetings; most sat silent. Then a tall man with a big presence joined the circle and sat, relaxed, waiting for everyone to settle.

After introductions, Chadwick made an invitation to the group—a dare, really—to "speak from the heart." (Where had I heard that before?) I wondered why there were no representatives of the Karuk, Yurok, Hoopa Valley, or Klamath Tribes in the circle, since he seemed to promise the type of conversation that the tribes of the Klamath watershed had long wanted. Consensus building begins, Chadwick told us, with willingness. While everyone present had strong opinions shaped by decades of conflict over water policy in the Klamath region, he encouraged the group to be willing to listen to one another's stories with an open heart. In the theatre, a similar willingness is required of audience and performers; we call it "the willing suspension of disbelief." We enter into an imaginative world, engage our muscles of empathy, set aside our doubts and judgments, and we come for a time into relation with others. For a short time we imagine that the characters we see on stage could be us. Chadwick was asking the group to take a similar leap of faith, one that also depended more on imagination and heart than on clever arguments and snazzy presentations. Can we imagine a reality in which community is possible, in which people, farms, and fish thrive?

I was struck by the number of agency and organizational acronyms used by participants at the session, and by the complexity of the legal morass that governed land, water, people, and fish in the Klamath watershed. Jurisdictional webs were thick as a blanket of fog over the valley. The historic divide between the federal Departments of the Interior and Agriculture seemed to be playing out before me. Officials from city, county, state, and federal agencies were often at cross-purposes. Older associations, like irrigation districts with long histories of local rule, resented governmental layers preempting their authority. Add to the mix the ad hoc citizen groups, environmental organizations, and tribal governments, together with long histories of broken treaties, contested boundaries and violence: the bureaucratic soup seemed like a toxic brew. Many people at the gathering complained that these very layers of jurisdiction were part of what made collaborating on the fate of fish so difficult. How could people begin to work together, much less see their subtle role in the ecology of the watershed, if they were tied up in such a web? By the end of the day my brain was full of alphabet soup. That evening I sat with a man from Oregon Fish and Wildlife and asked him to help me make sense of the long string of acronyms I'd heard during the day. Later this translated into the character of the Politician, who in scene 12 delivers an overly rehearsed PowerPoint that runs amok in agency logos and causes her to lose her cool.

That night I slept out under the stars in a lounge chair. Lying awake looking at the vivid Milky Way above, I found myself thinking that all of us—Upper Klamath farmers and ranchers, and the Yurok and Karuk people I'd met in Humboldt County—looked up at the same starry night. I remembered childhood night walks at family camp in which my mother pointed out constellations and explained the phenomenon of the Milky Way and the North Star. I imagined a scene in which a Klamath elder and a rancher looked up at the night sky together, and what they might say to one another. The next morning I jotted down notes for what later became that scene 19.

On the second day, the stakes were high and the circle was charged with emotion as farmers and ranchers told their stories and shared their frustrations. A Klamath Project farmer was angry: How dare the government—the same government that bid his immigrant parents to be part of a new agricultural development in the West in 1906—tell him that his hard work and that of his parents had to stop because of a fish?![36] He felt like he was being run off his own land by the "God Squad" (a nickname for the EPA). A woman from Oregon's commercial fishing community told us about her family's loss of livelihood. Her story was remarkably similar to those I had heard from Native people on the Lower Klamath. Story after story emerged, and as I looked around the circle, something was shifting. These stakeholders were becoming neighbors; real people, more than abstractions to one another and to me. Like many of my collaborators downriver, I had conflated this diverse and economically complicated community into a generalized enemy. I wanted the KTP group to meet these people and hear their stories, and I wanted these people to hear Yurok and Karuk stories. One thing that everyone at the Chadwick session seemed to agree on: solutions must be local, rooted in a respect for and knowledge of their long-standing relationship with the land itself—a value I knew Native people shared.

WIDENING THE CIRCLE

Back on campus I ran into Lauren and told her about the stakeholder meeting I'd attended and suggested she attend the next one, which would be held in Scott Valley. Lauren's first response was "no way!" Like many of the Native women in the KTP group, Lauren was shy and unaccustomed to speaking in public. In addition, she was a single mother and had no child care or funds for gas to drive the 150 miles. I told Lauren that the meeting needed her voice, that the people from the Upper Klamath that I'd heard seemed sincere and wanted to hear the lower river tribal perspectives from downriver. If she was willing to go, I'd find the money. I called Phil at the ITEPP office, and Terry Morton, who worked with Chadwick, and we were able to pull together some funding so that Lauren could attend. That she did was entirely an expression of her own courage. Lauren was the first Yurok from the Lower Klamath to attend one of the Chadwick sessions, and she returned on fire, saying, "I learned more than I thought possible! I met farmers and ranchers, BOR [Bureau of Reclamation] people, and commercial fishing families." Her stereotypes were broken. "These agencies and water users from upriver who we have been directing our anger at are actually just real people . . . people I genuinely like. . . . We should be working together, instead of just being insulted that the tribes might have to consider the economic loss that our needs might cause for those upriver." A Bureau of Reclamation official had offered to let Lauren stay at her house. "Talk about getting in with the enemy!" Lauren laughed. "She was awesome. I have so much hope now! That meeting was one of the best times I've had!" Lauren's experience enabled her to return with a clear vision for the play. "Both sides need to be represented. We have so much to learn from each other's perspectives. . . . Our audience is us *and* them—the people who don't understand each other, the cowboys and the Indians!"[37]

Lauren's presence at the Scott Valley session created an opening. Terry Morton phoned me to say that Lauren had helped the Chadwick team make a connection to the leadership of the Yurok Tribe. The next stakeholders session was held at the Yurok Tribal Headquarters in Klamath, California. For the first time in the present conflict many Yurok and Karuk fisheries personnel, tribal leaders, elders, and community members attended the session, sat in the circle, and spoke from the heart as farmers and ranchers from the Upper Klamath listened. I thought back to the audience's recommendation at our first concert reading a year earlier, in which elders envisioned farmers and ranchers coming downriver to eat salmon and hear their stories. Here was that longed-for table. Lauren had helped make that happen, and her story demonstrates the way in which the process of community-based theatre can activate communicative democracy.

THE BASIN

The next Chadwick session was held in Tule Lake, California, but in order to get there I had to drive through Oregon history. State Highway 66 between Ashland and Klamath Falls, Oregon, follows the old Applegate Trail—the road used by settlers who first came to the Klamath Basin from the west. The road winds up the lush western side of the Siskiyous and then crests with a dramatic change in climatic zones. Cedars, Douglas-firs, maples, and the dense underbrush of fern, salal, Oregon grape, and huckleberry are replaced by yellow pine, madrone, and manzanita; shafts of sunlight warm the spaces between them. As the road began to descend into the Klamath Basin,

I stopped to look at the valley opening up below me. Dry air filled my lungs and the smell of pine needles underfoot reminded me of the mountains of southern California where I'd grown up. Below, I could see the large serpentine river that lay at the center of so much heartache and vitriol. The Klamath Basin stretches north to the tributary Sprague and Williamson Rivers, which feed into the Klamath River near Chiloquin. The city of Klamath Falls, where in 2001 farmers and townspeople lined the streets in a "bucket brigade" to protest the EPA's ruling to protect the Klamath coho salmon, sits farther south at the confluence of the Lost River and the Klamath River. Lava Beds National Monument forms the southern end of the Klamath Basin. From a distance I could see the valley's expansive vernal marshlands that had provided ample hunting and fishing for the people who had lived there since time immemorial, and I could imagine that to the newcomers these lands had looked ripe for agriculture—provided the water could be controlled.

The session was held in an old hunting lodge, complete with deer, moose, and other animal heads on the walls. Sepia and black-and-white photos of fishing parties who had "caught the big one," fish or fowl, and nostalgic family photos of early-twentieth-century homesteaders lined the hallways and dining room walls. No mention, however, that Tule Lake was also the site of one of the US internment camps for Japanese Americans during World War II. After I stored my gear and said hello to people I'd met at previous meetings, I went for a walk. A trail across the road led out into high grasses and willow stands and then into a system of irrigation channels that carried water from a large pond out into fields of alfalfa that seemed to go on forever. I walked the berm between the channels. Looking south to the horizon, before my eye was forced upward by rugged mountains, I could make out a low, jagged band of black lava beds, and I made a mental note to visit the park while I was in the area.

At dinner I sat down at a table with Becky Hatfield Hyde, who had come to the session with her children and husband. I thanked her for an essay she had written that had come over the Klamath watershed e-mail list some months earlier. The Hyde family's Yamsi Ranch on the Williamson River in Chiloquin is one of the oldest in the basin, dating back several generations. Part of the next generation, and having witnessed firsthand the devastating social and ecological impact of conflict in the Klamath Basin, Becky Hatfield Hyde and Taylor Hyde purchased another ranch with the intention of charting a new course. The 788-acre Yainix Ranch, near the confluence of the Sprague and the Sycan Rivers, had suffered severe environmental degradation from years of overgrazing and neglect. Becky and Taylor Hyde now operate Yainix as a conservation easement in cooperation with the Klamath Tribes and are working to make the ranch a model of sustainable practice.[38] Yainix Ranch, Becky told me, "works to educate both Native kids and white kids in land stewardship." She also said, "Change is hard. But we can either go with it or fight it; but either way, all of us are going to have to give up something." Like the young Native women I knew, Becky Hyde was committed, engaged, rooted in the land, and *she wasn't going anywhere*. The efforts of the Hatfield Hyde family would inspire the characters of Tim and Alice—a hopeful young rancher with deep family ties to the land, and his mother, who is tired of the long years of conflict. Like their real-world counterparts in the Upper Klamath, Tim and Alice love the land enough to be changed by it.

PRAYER TIME

The next day I drove to Lava Beds National Monument. I could see the craggy black outline on the southern horizon, but the drive was longer than I thought, through miles of irrigated fields: no barns, no homes, no buildings in sight. I knew I'd entered the national monument area when the pavement changed from truck-worn, pitted asphalt to newly paved blacktop with a fresh centerline: federal dollars at work, I thought. I passed a turnout on the left where a white wooden cross and a circle of parking spaces drew the visitor in. An engraved plaque told of the cavalry's battle with the Modocs in 1873, and General Canby's death at the hands of Captain Jack, a Modoc warrior and political leader. Ironically, Captain Jack has become a folk hero in the Klamath Basin, as farmers and ranchers began to identify their own struggle for survival with that of the group of Modocs that the US government massacred over a century ago. My mind struggled to make sense of history and the ways in which it is remembered and invoked.

I drove on to the next visitor turnout. No markers invited inspection, but a trail guide offered a nature walk up into the lava rocks, with descriptions of flora and fauna and a narrative of the Modoc resistance that occurred there. I picked my way among formations a half-million years old, part of the Medicine Lake shield volcano. Similar lava fields can be found near the many volcanic peaks in the Cascades—Mount Saint Helens, Crater Lake, Mount Lassen. The sharp protrusions seemed like newly formed crystalline gobs, strange black shapes, sharp as broken glass to the touch. Sage and dry grass found footholds in the cracks and crevices where bits of soil, deposited by wind, had given life its only purchase. The precarious rootedness and determined tenacity of the shrubs reminded me of the farmers and ranchers who were trying to hold on while change blew in heaps around them. As I traced a random path over an ancient and violent eruption, I looked back to see the vast Klamath Basin stretching northward—the largest flyway for migratory birds in the West.[39] From this wide angle, the land forms a large, shallow lakebed, a huge sump. Tule Lake fills with water in winter and spring and then recedes in summer—a kind of inland tide that allowed life and Modoc culture to flourish for thousands of years.

Captain Jack, accompanied by fifty warriors and their families, fled into these rocks for final refuge. They were able to fight off four hundred cavalrymen for six months. The rock had their backs, but it was the water, which in the wetter months comes up to the edge of the lava beds, that allowed them to survive. Ghosts seemed to fly out of the weird formations. There, I imagined elders, women, and children huddled together against the rock; there, a place deep enough for men to stand and shoot; and there, some soft sand between two lava walls where a mother might allow her child some freedom of movement. A chipmunk scurried into and then out of my view; a lizard basked in the sun. I wondered what the Modoc women said to their children. "Everything will be okay"? "Pray to Creator for protection"? "Eat this, it's all we have"? The cavalry finally succeeded in overtaking the Modocs by cutting off their access to the water in Tule Lake. And then change rolled into the valley like a volcanic eruption, fueled not by geologic forces but by greed, opportunism, and the newcomers' desire to stake their claim on the land. That I was a descendant of newcomers like these (though mine had settled in the Missouri Territory) was not lost on me as I contemplated how life had changed in the Klamath Basin over the past two hundred years.

I sat down on a small piece of soil, wiggling in so that the sharp rock was not sticking me in the ribs, and I made a small watercolor of an odd black butte that rose directly to the east, surrounded by golden fields. I would learn later from Gordon Bettles that Schonchin Butte marks the intersection of the east-west Applegate Trail and the California-Oregon route, which served gold miners pushing north and south. Named for a Modoc chief who fought alongside Captain Jack, the butte has been the site of numerous atrocities and violent encounters in the clash of cultures of the two last centuries. My watercolor became a kind of meditation, as I worked a pale wash over the paper, adding shapes in red, green, yellow, and black, letting the colors run together. Thinking about the families that had been forced to hide among these jagged rocks, tears streamed down my face. I put the brush down and prayed. Now more than ever, I was aware of the magnitude of loss that had occurred on this land, the gnarled layers of injury and injustice, and the deep-rooted convictions that masked that history as "progress." I understood myself as a product of that history, felt insignificant and humbled by what I knew and did not know but was working hard to learn—not only from people but from the land. My prayer went something like this: "Let me be useful here. Help me write a play that contributes to healing, that echoes in a good way the voices I've heard."

Later I wrote a version of my visit to the Lava Beds National Monument as scene 18. I imagined the character of Tim driving in to Klamath Falls for supplies, and then, on a whim, out to the lava beds for some time alone with his thoughts. Torn between his loyalty to the land, his family's values, and his new understanding of the needs of the larger watershed community in which he lives, Tim sits and has a smoke. Maybe he tells the audience about Captain Jack and the Modoc resistance. As he contemplates his geographic and historic sense of place, Tim has a change of heart. He decides to embrace his complicated history with a willingness to put community first. But before he leaves, he tosses some tobacco from his pouch onto the ground—a gesture of reverence he learned from his Klamath-Modoc neighbors.

NEW COLLABORATORS

As some students involved in the project graduated, new students, Native and non-Native, theatre trained and not, joined the project. They brought fresh energy and added their own voices to our discussions of the issues; they conducted additional interviews and research that contributed to the form and content of the play-in-progress. One of these new collaborators was Kathleen McCovey, a graduate student in an environmental humanities seminar that I taught. She had returned to school as part of her work to document and preserve the ecological knowledge and cultural traditions of the Karuk people.

In the seminar, Kathy told us a story about hunting with her grandfather and taking her first deer. "I kept that deer hide in my freezer for years!" she said. After her grandfather passed, she tanned the hide and made a ceremonial skirt, decorating it with shells she had collected on the beach. The skirt seemed to have a palpable presence. It seemed to speak as Kathy held it to her body, and the sound of the ocean rose up like a song as she walked across the room. After class I told Kathy about *Salmon Is Everything* and asked if she would be part of the project as a cultural adviser and collaborator. She eagerly accepted and quickly became an invaluable asset in the development of the script toward performance. "But," she warned me with a twinkle in her eye, "I'm not going to get up on a stage!"

We were scheduled to present a reading of our play-in-progress at Humboldt State's annual Week of Dialogue on Race, with a new role drawn from Kathy's story. Even though she had told me she didn't want to perform, I gave her a copy of the script, hoping that she would at least consider being part of the reading. After all, some of these were her words. It's not really acting, I told her, it's just reading. She laughed in her big-hearted way and agreed to read the role of Rose. Inspired by Kathy, several of the other Native women students also agreed to be part of the reading.

In the discussion that followed this reading, Native students talked with Latino, black, and LGBTQ students about environmental justice, building stronger connections between the university's Native students and those in other historically marginalized groups. The reading helped put Native concerns nearer the center of the university's ongoing discussions of equity and diversity. After the reading, a colleague who identifies as queer suggested that the emerging characters of Kate and Rachel, a gay couple, were a laudable effort at inclusion, but she thought their relationship muddied the Indigenous issues at the center of the play. I considered taking her recommendation to cut the relationship out of the play, but first I went to talk with Sue Burcell. "No, don't you dare!" Sue said. "Queer identity is as important in Native culture as it is in any culture. Native people also need to be more tolerant."

In addition to the several public and university readings during the development of *Salmon Is Everything*, I took copies of the play-in-progress to the Chadwick stakeholder gathering at Yurok Headquarters in Klamath. After one of the evening meals, I invited a handful of session participants to read various roles, while other attendees listened. Response to this informal reading indicated that the play was beginning to tell the multiple stories of this watershed community. The play was beginning to function as a bridge.

SMALL ACTS OF REPAIR

The spiritual and cultural significance of salmon continued to be the most important thematic element for my collaborators, and we spent many hours talking about how to communicate this idea to a non-Native audience. One April day I was helping a friend prepare food for Passover. We began talking about the ways in which food is central in all religious traditions. "This is one of the primary Judaic ceremonies, and it's all about food!" I'd met Nicole Barchilon Frank during a theatre project in which her daughter had been involved, and through our long friendship I had learned much about Jewish traditions—knowledge that helped me make sense of many of the Catholic practices I'd learned as a child. I knew that the Mass, for example, is modeled on Passover, but I had not understood the specific symbolic and ecological meanings of the *matzah*, the cup of wine for Elijah, the bitter herbs, the sweet and salty tastes. "Each of these foods has a story to tell that reminds us who we are," she said. Like the ceremonial meals of the First Salmon, the foods of the Mass and the Passover nourish body and spirit and remind us of our interconnection with the earth. Nicole's joyous kitchen of edible spirits inspired the idea to give each of the three family groups in the play a food-based expression of faith as a way to show that salmon, like the Passover meal and Catholic Communion, is at the center of a spiritual practice as well as a cultural identity. By including Jewish as well as Christian religious practices in the play, I hoped that non-Native audience members might come closer to understanding the sacred nature of Indigenous people's relationship with the salmon.

Nicole is a dedicated scholar of Judaic philosophies and ancient texts, and she often bolstered my spirits when I got discouraged. "Rabbi Zalman Schachter-Shalomi says that the Universe is like a grand fabric, like a garment.[40] The Hebrew letters for universe and for garment are similar. See?" She drew the ancient shapes with her finger. "The garment is torn everywhere by all the rapes and violence, the injustice and pollution, the cruelty and war in the world. Rabbi Zalman says that what our lives are about"—she took her own skirt in her hands—"is mending a small part of that torn fabric." In the blue-green print of her skirt I could see the tender world spinning in space, a tapestry of communities and ecologies rich and textured, and yes, torn. In scene 10, Rachel (inspired by Nicole's words) reminds Kate that ecological and social justice must be understood as spiritual concerns.

WEAVING THE PLAY[41]

At the end of the academic year some KTP students were graduating, and others were leaving school for family and work reasons; community members were departing for the river for summer fishing and ceremonies. It was time for assessing how far we had come and what might be next for the project. We had amassed a sizable body of material that recorded the feelings of the Native communities about the fish kill. We had shared that material publicly in many settings. In preparation for each of our concert readings, I had already begun weaving together the many voices and styles present in our material. I'd begun fleshing out thematic ideas and developing composite characters and potential narrative threads, but the text was far from a play. Before I continued writing, I needed the group's direction.

At our last meeting of the year, I talked with the group about the process of play-making. While I had certain skills and knowledge most of my collaborators did not, the play that I would ultimately weave out of our joint research and creative work needed to reflect the sensibilities and priorities of my collaborators. I asked them to describe what they thought the play should look like, sound like, feel like. What did they most want the play to communicate? "The anger!" said one of the young men in the group, and then a cacophony of voices followed as each one called out what should be at the heart of the play. "Yes, the feelings, how we felt, the sadness." "How we relate to the salmon. How it's part of our family, that it's what we feed our babies." "How the elders took it so personally, that look in my Gram's eyes." Others chimed in. "The play's got to communicate what our culture is really like, the dip net fishing and our ceremonies." "Yes, and that the salmon are spiritual to us. It's not like food from McDonald's, like some kid said to me in class the other day. *That* needs to be in the play!" As their playwright, I told them, this information about what they wanted the play to say was exactly what I needed to know.

I asked how they felt about the composite characters I'd begun to develop, in which dialogue was composed from several different interviews and combined into a fictional relationship. Should I continue in this direction, or should we use the actual identities of the people whose stories we had gathered? Ultimately, they agreed that fictional characters allowed for the stories to be personal while still preserving the anonymity of the original tellers. We talked about the idea of "plot" and I asked how they felt about using some of their own experiences working on this project as the basis for a story line: Lauren going to the stakeholder meeting, for example, or scenes based on some of our adventures together. The group affirmed this strategy, saying that our times together, and the many ways we had grown as people, were some of the most fun and interesting aspects of the project. I proposed that I work with the material over the summer and return in the fall with a working draft that reflected their decisions. Then what? they asked. I explained the typical process of play development in which actors test how the scenes play through a workshop rehearsal process. As we hear how the dialogue sounds and see what action and characters seem believable or not, we make more revisions, and so on. Working the play in this way allows the actors to help shape the final product. We agreed on this strategy for the following year, and then, because I knew some of the group would not return in the fall, we went around the circle and acknowledged each member's contribution before saying good-bye.

The dramatic structure of *Salmon Is Everything* grew out of the challenges we faced as a collaborative group as much as it did from our research into the issues and events. It would not be a play with a single cohesive plot; it would always struggle to find its voice through many voices. I distilled the material we had collected and written into three family groups: a young Yurok woman, her Karuk husband, and her extended family; a rancher and his elderly mother; and a graduate student fish biologist and her partner. The narrative would follow the journey of Julie, a Yurok woman, caught between her own family and community's rage and grief after the fish kill, and her growing friendship with an Upper Klamath rancher. Lauren's experience going to the stakeholder meeting provided a narrative thread that would link the diverse interviews, monologues, characters, and situations. The play would continue to change over the course of rehearsals the following year. Those rehearsals—up to minutes before opening the doors for the audience—were an ongoing negotiation with the same questions that had rung in my mind over the previous two years of development: How do we honor those we represent? How do we share knowledge? How do all of us allow space for the histories that haunt us?

A friend familiar with the fraught and sometimes bitter politics of the Klamath watershed recently asked me why the non-Native characters in the play—specifically Tim, Alice, and Kate—were treated with such generosity. Indeed, some of the conflicts I observed and overheard in the watershed at the time of the 2002 fish kill might have merited stronger antagonists to realistically reflect the politically polarized community. Yet, play-making is always a balance between reporting on what is and conjuring what might be. The vitriol expressed in the slashing of Kate's tires in scene 14 was entirely plausible at the time, while the selfless act of a rancher offering to pay for Kate's new tires in that scene is certainly an act of fiction. Meanwhile, Kate's character development from an ignorant but well-meaning, nature-loving environmentalist into a more thoughtful ally, who has a place in her scientific world view for traditional ecological knowledge, is a transformation that surely takes a lifetime, not a single season. Given the history of the watershed—the backstory for these characters—perhaps my depictions are too generous.

While drama often claims to "hold up a mirror" to life, its job is also to provide a vision of what might be, to open possibilities of being, ways of seeing the world, and to suggest relationships that challenge who we are and who we might become. Characters also serve as invitations. As they move through changes that seem improbable, the characters demonstrate a process of transformation that grows out of willingness not only to consider other points of view, but to come into relation with others and be changed by them. My colleague Gordon Bettles, who wrote the foreword to this volume, often teaches a Klamath greeting song that translates "I change you, you change me." The characters of Tim and Alice were inspired by some of the farmers and ranchers in the Upper Klamath who are working to live in good relations with their tribal neighbors, to work collaboratively toward fair and equitable agricultural practices that honor both ecology and cultures. The characters modeled on them are invitations, spaces through which members of the audience, readers, or future production teams might also come into relation, allowing themselves to be changed by the characters in the play and by one another. Relationship has risks, but in order to heal the past and build a just and sustainable future, the play suggests, we must take them—as Tim does at the end of the play. The scene in which Tim calls Julie, declares his solidarity, and promises to "tell the others" is intended to conjure an alternative future: one in which Tim's real world counterparts on the river have Julie and Will's counterparts on speed-dial; one in which Rose and Alice's counterparts regularly swap stories of their grandchildren, trade blackberry jam and smoked salmon recipes. (Indeed, as scene 20 alludes, in the years of activism since the fish kill of 2002, the tribes on the Klamath River have renewed the Annual Salmon Run along 260 miles of spawning grounds.)[42] In this way the characters embody the hope of a watershed in which all residents regard one another with a spirit of generosity, one in which rhetorical, legal, and material weapons give way to a co-imagined future, a watershed in which everyone thrives.

These non-Native characters also reflect the generosity of the Native students, colleagues, and community members with whom I worked on this project. Their generosity to *me* in moments that I said, did or suggested something in ignorance is reflected in many of the primary characters in the play. In these learning moments, even when my inherited privilege was writ large, my collaborators always gave me the benefit of the doubt. My collaborators' willingness to come into relation with me allowed me to be changed by them.

CASTING

In the fall, I coordinated with Sue Burcell and Phil Zastrow about how to enter into this new phase of the project in which we needed actors—or at least people willing to take such a risk. Even as I reserved the studio theatre on campus and began to think about casting, I was aware of a new set of challenges. Many Native people are suspicious of theatre for good reasons. Historically, theatre has been complicit in the oppression of Native peoples. Frontier plays, theatrical events like the Wild West Show, and so-called anthropological exhibitions at various World's Fairs of the nineteenth and twentieth centuries manufactured and perpetuated stereotypes that helped construct a rationale for acts of genocide. I knew that to avoid reinscribing this history, the Native roles in the play must be played by Native actors, whether they had theatre experience or not. But unlike the invitation to write and help document events in their communities, the opportunity to perform in a play was not as appealing to Native young people. "We're not used to taking center stage," Sue reminded me. "Our young people learn to be respectful, rather than speaking out or grabbing attention." Even though many in the group had by now read the play-in-progress aloud in public, "acting" presented a different challenge.

Happily, two Native colleagues who had been supportive advisers from the beginning, Marlon Sherman and Phil Zastrow, were willing to be role models. Phil had acted and sung in many community musicals and was delighted to be in a play about Native people, especially one that some of his students and community had helped write. Marlon had been part of the concert readings of the play the year before, but a production represented a larger commitment. As professor of Native American studies, Marlon teaches film criticism courses that deconstruct the very representations of Native people that I was worried about. When I asked him if he'd consider acting in the play, Marlon looked over his shoulder as if haunted by those ghosts of history and then grinned and said, "Well, okay." Hurray! I threw my arms around both of them.

The task of finding actors was a reminder that in community-based projects, outreach must be ongoing. I began talking with people, visiting and talking to classes, meeting new ITEPP students, calling everyone I knew who might be connected in the various communities, and making coffee dates to talk with people. Slowly a company of players emerged. Mary Campbell was a Native studies major and member of the Hoopa Valley Tribe, and she had acting experience. As part of the team that had recently prepared cultural objects from northern California tribes for the new wing of the Smithsonian Museum in Washington, DC, Mary was keenly aware of the kind of representation that our play must work against. When it came time to begin rehearsals, I still did not have several roles filled. I was most worried about finding an elder to play Rose, the character inspired by Kathy McCovey. I trusted that if we simply began rehearsing, the right people would hear about the project and find their way to us.

As our cultural adviser on the play, Kathy came to rehearsals regularly. This was her community's story. She helped us get the cultural details right, corrected inflections in language, and helped shape onstage action by giving actors suggestions about what the Native characters would be doing at home. "But don't try to get me up there performing," she reiterated. "I can't talk in front of groups!" After some weeks, however, Kathy announced that she would indeed play the role of Rose. Cheers went up in rehearsal that day! I knew this was no small gift of time and nerve. She was a full-time student and a tribal leader, worked full-time, and had family obligations. Others came too, having heard by word of mouth about the project: Robin Andrews (Rosebud Sioux), finishing her bachelor's degree; and children of Mary Risling (Karuk), who works with Native students at Humboldt State. I recruited a local retired professional actor to play Tim and filled the other non-Native roles with students and community members who had come to auditions. But I still did not have a young man to play the role of Will, the Yurok subsistence fisherman and Julie's husband. We began to rehearse without this central character. One day a young Karuk man walked into the studio in the middle of rehearsal and announced, "My dad told me I should come to see about being in the play." This was Jason Reed, the son of Ron Reed, cultural biologist for the Karuk fisheries department and an international leader and organizer for the fate of Klamath salmon. Jason had never acted before, but he told me that he wanted to do it "for the fish." We handed him a copy of the play and he jumped in with gusto, exclaiming, "I'm going to pretend to be my dad, so look out!"

Jason brought his cousin to the next rehearsal. "Can he be in the play too?" the young men asked, and thus the character of Johnny was born. While I am not recommending that characters be added to a play for the sake of including everyone, I am advocating that artists working in community keep certain questions open: What would these new voices bring to our collective process? What knowledge might they share that will ignite new understanding in the others (including me) or in our eventual audience? Casting *Salmon Is Everything* taught me that the process of community outreach and inclusion never stops—not once the play is written; not after rehearsals begin; not at dress rehearsal; not even after the show opens. The door must remain open.

BUILDING ENSEMBLE

I anticipated that rehearsals would bring many changes to the dialogue and sometimes the structure of scenes. So that I could spend more time listening, writing, and making revisions in rehearsal, I asked Jean O'Hara to codirect. Our first task was to create a rehearsal schedule devised around everyone's schedules. The resulting matrix told actors the days and times we would rehearse the scenes in which they appeared, and thus when they were to be at rehearsal. Typically, we rehearsed in the afternoon from 4 to 7 p.m., in the gap between work and classes, between dinner, homework, and parenting duties.

Despite our organization, actors seemed to attend rehearsal randomly, on any day they had free, but not always on the day they were called. Often actors came one or two hours late, giving the project what time they could afford that day. I recalled my frustrations about time and absences from the early days of the project, and after a day or two I suggested to Jean, "Let's throw out the schedule and work with who shows up."

Flexibility allowed us to respond to the changing needs of our community of players, but it also quickly created an ensemble. As soon as anyone arrived, we rehearsed the scenes that person happened to be in. If two actors were there who were in a scene, any scene, we rehearsed that scene. If four actors were there, but only two actors from a multiperson scene were present, we asked the other actors to play the missing roles. This kept us on our toes creatively and produced a fluid and spontaneous collaborative atmosphere. By the time the show opened, every actor had rehearsed and knew well several other roles in the play! If an actor missed a rehearsal or a performance (which happened), another actor could easily pick up that role. It also allowed everyone to be part of the whole, to understand the arc of the play, to make connections between scenes, and to make suggestions not only about his or her own character and dialogue but about other roles as well. Our Native collaborators corrected facts, inflections, and characterizations. Working this way deepened each actor's sense of ownership. We had become an ensemble, a company of players, weaving the process of play-making with building community.

The rehearsal process added details to the play as individual actors shared cultural knowledge and skills with the ensemble. Teaching moments were plentiful and often disarming. As Kathy developed the role of Rose, she began to bring basket-making materials to rehearsal. She told us about the bear grass and willow roots and explained how Karuk women make colors from the black stem of the five-finger fern, and dye bear grass bright yellow by soaking it in wolf lichen. She explained other medicinal herbs and talked about Karuk beliefs in which everything has a spirit. Kathy wrote down what she'd taught us and I incorporated it into scene 11. She also helped revise other stories in the script in order to more fully communicate Karuk traditions. We talked about incorporating her Brush Dance skirt into the play, perhaps as part of a scene with the women. She brought it to rehearsal, and I provided a basket for her to lay it in. "What's that for?" she asked me. "Well, wouldn't Rose keep her skirt in a basket, or . . . ?" Kathy laughed and said, "Well, no, actually. *These days* we keep them in rolling carry-on suitcases! That way you can toss them easily into the back of a pickup when you're going to ceremony." We all laughed until our sides hurt as I realized the unconscious stereotype in my suggestion.

LIVING OBJECTS

In much the same way that non-Native people might not understand the spiritual significance of the salmon, we may also miss the distinction between objects of material culture and our own everyday possessions. I wrote a scene in which the character of Rose shows her Brush Dance skirt to Kate and Rachel. As I first wrote it, Rachel, entranced by the skirt's beauty and spiritual significance, takes the skirt and holds it up to her own body. When I brought this scene to rehearsal Kathy and Mary scoffed and said "No way! No, we can't do that! Rose would *never* let Rachel hold the skirt! She would never let anyone parade around with it! This is *living regalia*. The skirt *has danced* and only the woman who dances in it can touch it." Together the women set about rewriting the scene so that it was consistent with cultural values and protocol. This kind of cross-cultural knowledge sharing not only enriched every member of the group, it directly informed our creative product. We then translated my learning moment into stage action: when the character of Rachel (not knowing what I now knew) reaches for the skirt, Rose quickly pulls it away. Then the character of Julie explains why.

I had grown used to the presence of children at rehearsals. Several cast members did not have child care, or they were caring for someone else's children, and regularly brought them to rehearsal where the children did homework or watched. One evening during a break, while Jean and I were preoccupied, some of the children began playing with the stage props, including a cradleboard that had been brought from home by one of the elder cast members to use in certain scenes. The children began running around the stage, playing keep-away with the cradleboard. An elder watching the rehearsal that evening rose to her feet and shouted, "Stop that! That is not a toy!" Her voice was filled with emotion as she explained to me, "This is a cradleboard that we keep in our home, that our ancestors made, that we lay our babies in, that our grandbabies will lay in. It is a *living object*. It's disrespectful to treat it this way. It's not a prop!" I understood her concern as surely as if I'd seen my great-grandmother's china teapot being used in a sandbox. And yet, there is more. In the Karuk spiritual tradition, matter is not mere "stuff"—it is spirit filled. This is what Julie means when she says to Kate in scene 6, "My people [. . .] *are* the trees, the water, the fish. That the Salmon are brothers is not some kind of myth." Objects like the cradleboard are made from living things—willow, ash, hide, bone—by the hands of relatives who return to that same earth when they die, where they grow into the trees and bushes that feed the animals and the people. Perhaps if my great-grandmother's china teapot had not been made in an English factory but had instead been fashioned by her own mother out of ancestral bones, my analogy above might seem more apt. We decided to put a note in the production program explaining to the audience that some objects they see on stage are not "props" or "costumes," but rather living material culture, and are not to be touched by anyone except the actor that handles them—a note we recommend to anyone staging the play with regalia, or other objects of material culture.

Two hours before the performance was to begin, Kathy arrived and told me that she could not bring her dip net down from her home in Happy Camp as planned (a three-hour drive on a mountain road) because it was too big to get in her truck. This meant that Jason and Bobbie would not have a "real" dip net for scene 7. Jean and I attempted to make-shift a replacement using a long stick with some burlap netting on the end. But the young men looked at me incredulously and laughed at the miserable prop—not even a good approximation of a dip net! By the time the stage manager had called "places," the men had scoured the campus landscape for long branches and, using netting from the back of someone's truck, constructed a real dip net—about five times the size of the prop I'd offered. Their faces beamed, and I was impressed not only by their knowledge and skill but by their commitment to the play, to telling the story, to getting it right.

The final scene of the play is intended to communicate a sense of the sacredness of the salmon, and the ways our human lives are so deeply connected to the earth through the land, the river, our families, and communities. The text came from a free-writing exercise in which I'd asked the group to write about the meaning of the word "sacred." In response they said, "We don't have a word like that in Yurok. We don't need it. Everything is sacred, but we don't say it." Another said, "There's no word in Karuk either." I realized that the word in English signals a binary that allows for its opposite, "secular," exposing a worldview in which only some things, places, and people are sacred. For my Native collaborators, however, sacred was just the way it was. Two students who were learning Karuk and Yurok from their elders told us that the closest translation was "in a good way" or "with a good heart." As the lights dimmed and the stage darkened, these voices in Yurok, Karuk, Hupa, and English overlapped, echoed, and merged with the sound of the river.

EMPATHY AS POLITICAL ACTION

One of the most frequent questions I receive about *Salmon Is Everything* is, "Did it make any difference?" The question whether theatre (or any art) matters is important not only because artists and activists want their work to contribute to social change, but also because answering this question helps us understand *how* theatre participates in civic discourse—how it matters. In an article on the social power of theatre, Jill Dolan observes that the "actor's willing vulnerability perhaps enables our own and prompts us toward compassion and greater understanding. Such sentiments can spur our emotion, and being moved emotionally is a necessary precursor to political movement."[43] Theatre's primary function is not necessarily to change laws or policies, but to provide a forum in which people might imaginatively share in one another's experience. Witnessing a play, a person might ponder questions such as, What if that was my grandmother's experience? What if that happened to my child? What if I felt that humiliation, fear, or rage? Theatre is a unique art form because it takes place before our eyes, in and with our flesh-and-blood presence. A living forum, theatre invites us not only to think about how others might feel, but to *feel into* those possibilities in real time in the company of others. In this way it lays down new fibers of community in the form of relationships as well as stories. This is how the play mattered. Those fibers of relatedness include not only the diverse and complicated communities of the Klamath River watershed, but all those who have worked or will work on productions of this play, its audiences, and now, you.

THE JOURNEY HOME

Jean O'Hara

By emphasizing the public, rather than the private, repercussions of traumatic violence and loss, social actors turn personal pain into the engine for cultural change.

Diana Taylor[44]

In 1995 I moved to Wiyot land, or what is now called northern California. The following winter was the first time I encountered a live salmon in its natural environment. It was late December and I was helping a member of the Watershed Stewards record the number of salmon and redds (gravel spawning nests) along Freshwater Creek. It wasn't long before we came upon a huge magenta and silver female salmon protecting her redd. She frightened both of us with her quick, loud movement, letting us know we were in her territory. Farther up the creek we found another female preparing her redd as two males fought over who would release his semen on her eggs; the bigger salmon won.

Later that spring, I was invited to volunteer for the annual salmon census along the Salmon River, one of the tributaries of the Klamath River. I spent an entire day in a thick wetsuit and snorkel, floating downriver counting salmon, amazed by their grace and strength as they swam upstream against the currents. The experience of being carried downstream by the river for hours, the images of strong-bodied salmon, flashing silver in the water, are as vivid to me today as they were that day seventeen years ago.

At one point along the river, I came face-to-face with a large chinook salmon with a particularly intimidating set of teeth. Despite knowing the salmon would never harm me, I instinctively pulled my head out of the water. By the end of the day, my crew had counted over one hundred salmon on a two-mile section of river. Little did I know that a mere six years later, the experience that my crew and I had enjoyed that day would come under threat. Little did I know that day that while I had no reason to fear the salmon, the salmon had every reason to fear my kind, and me.

My first encounter with the play *Salmon Is Everything* was at the first concert reading. Theresa asked me to listen, to share my own impressions, and to take notes on the community discussion that followed. After the reading and discussion, I was struck by the potency of the storytelling and the potential for this medium to address a complex community crisis. This very first audience became what Diana Taylor calls "co-owners": "Bearing witness is a live process, a doing, and event that takes place in real time, in the presence of a listener who comes to be a participant and a co-owner of the traumatic event." I initially accepted Theresa's invitation to collaborate simply thinking I would help the salmon, without recognizing their important relationship to the Hupa, Karuk, and Yurok communities. As an Irish American, I began to realize that I didn't have a clear understanding of the worldviews of each of these three nations. What I learned in this process and later through the rehearsals and performances was how integral and interwoven the salmon are in every facet of life for the Hupa, Karuk, and Yurok people. I began to understand the enormity of loss my Native friends and community were experiencing.

Throughout the development of the play, my role alternated between recorder and actor. In the spring of 2006, Theresa invited me to codirect the production of *Salmon is Everything*. My background in ensemble theatre matched Theresa's collaborative approach, and codirecting with her was a dynamic and rewarding experience. One of my favorite aspects of the rehearsal and production process was the sense of humor that was brought into the space. Robin Andrews (Lakota) would actually lead us in a "laugh circle." Mary Campbell (Hupa) would call Marlon Sherman (Lakota) "Wind in the Hair." Everyone cracked jokes at any opportunity. I led the cast in a number of songs and movement warm-ups that were goofy at best. Humor has always been an important part of Native theatre and Native cultures. According to playwright William Yellow Robe Jr., "It's the humor that allows you to keep your sanity, and gives you the courage and strength to get through the pain." Or, as theatre artist Hanay Geiogamah says, "Humor is a blessing. And I see it as one of the fundamental miracles of our lives."[45] It was humor that allowed us to return, in each rehearsal and performance, to the story of the traumatic loss of the salmon.

On opening night, and in subsequent performances, we played to full houses. The positive responses and heartfelt dialogue following the performances surprised us. We created a space for potential healing while simultaneously galvanizing direct action. The dialogue continued outside the theatre space, when the entire cast, crew, and support staff came to my home for a potluck. We all celebrated as we shared food and stories. As the evening wound down, the remaining people were mostly cast members who were sitting in a circle on the floor in my apartment. People began to discuss their own stories and feelings connected to the issues raised in the play. Kathy McCovey told us that when she and her partner, Bryan Colegrove, had been out shopping that week, a group of teens had made fun of Bryan, pointing and jeering at the "Indian." Theresa talked about her experience of white privilege and guilt around her own ancestors' possible connection to the mistreatment of Native peoples. More than one Native person conveyed that guilt wasn't what they wanted. What they wanted was for the mistreatment to end. The conversation continued around racism, the US government, rights around spiritual practices, and what our visions were for the continuation of the Klamath Theatre Project. By the end of the evening a unanimous decision was made to bring *Salmon Is Everything* to the Hupa, Karuk, and Yurok Reservations. With no funding, summertime around the corner, and ceremonial dances about to begin, we decided to reconvene in the fall.

By the fall, Theresa had accepted a position at the University of Oregon, and I became the sole director. As a group we brainstormed ideas for potential funding, but by the end of fall we were able to raise only $2400 (half of this directly from Humboldt State president Rollin Richmond). Unlike the first production, which had been partially supported by Humboldt State's theatre department, the tour was not supported. This left us with no set, no stage manager, and no technical support. By spring 2007, we had also lost five actors of the original cast. However, through auditions, connections within the Native community, and a willingness to combine certain roles, we were able to assemble a cast and one assistant. Bubba (Glen) Sanchez, a Hupa, took on three roles, while Arianna McLennan, a Yurok, played the roles of two women. Another exciting addition to the cast was Sue Burcell's grandson, Ish-Kaysh Tripp. As it turned out, of this new cast, all the Native performers were from local tribes directly affected by the salmon kill. Other new additions were Nora Chatmon and Katie Skinner. Adrianna Guzman, a graduate student conducting research about *Salmon Is Everything*, also joined the production. Together we created a rehearsal and performance schedule, with the first performance slated for Humboldt State's Social Justice Summit.

After a successful full house production at the Social Justice Summit, we brought *Salmon Is Everything* to the Hupa, Yurok, and Karuk communities. What I appreciated about the touring process was how the simple production elements—just wooden boxes and the actors—brought the piece closer to traditional storytelling. The tour allowed for the integration of the performance with the land and people that ultimately held the story. Also, Native cast members had the opportunity to share their homes and communities with the rest of us. On the drive to Hoopa, Mary and Sam Campbell pointed out a beautiful stretch of land along the Trinity River where the Hupa salmon ceremony was traditionally held. They told us that Rob Arkley Sr., a local businessman, had won the land in a poker bet: a millionaire now owns the land where the Hupa performed their salmon ceremony for centuries. At that moment, I witnessed the lasting effects of the Dawes Act and other colonial acts that endeavored to break up Indigenous communal landholdings. In Hoopa, we performed at the high school, Mary and Bubba's alma mater. I learned that Hoopa Valley High School was built on the same site as the previous government-sponsored boarding school meant to force Native children to assimilate European language, customs, and worldviews. Mary Campbell shared that her grandmother had survived abuses at this boarding school.

Our next performance was at the Yurok Reservation. We visited the mouth of the Klamath River, site of the fish kill and the impetus for the play. Actor Adrianna McCleland pointed out the nearby sandbar where the Yurok ceremonial dances were held. Many of the non-Native actors had never seen the mouth of the Klamath, while some Native actors had never visited the north side of the river at the overlook. To our delight, a whale blew water out of her spout as we were taking group photos.

For our final performance, we drove the two-hour winding river road to Karuk country. Kathy and Bryan met us at Orleans Elementary School, where we were set to perform. Along the way, Kathy pointed out a Karuk ceremonial site. Months later I would be invited to a Brush Dance at that site, where I witnessed Bryan Colegrove and Phil Zastrow dance as part of the ceremony. Through the touring process, I experienced a remapping of this familiar landscape. My sense of place now included Indigenous history and understandings.

The Social Justice Summit production and the tour of *Salmon Is Everything* followed the format of the first production by inviting audience members to discuss the issues raised in the play. Adrianna Guzman also handed out feedback forms for audience members to fill out. One young Hupa man talked about how the performance helped him understand the connection that ranchers and farmers had with the land and their fears of losing their way of life. In *Performing as a Moral Act: Ethical Dimensions of the Ethnography of Performance*, Dwight Conquergood describes a dialogic performance as one that creates a "space between competing ideologies. It brings self and other together even while it holds them apart." *Salmon Is Everything*'s dialogic quality was evident in the post-play discussions. A Karuk elder shared some other environmental issues caused by water diversion and capitalism: willow roots have been damaged by low water levels, making them unusable for basket making, and wild mushrooms have been overharvested by non-Native people for profit. A Native woman shared how difficult the salmon kill was for her community, explaining that "after a funeral you wash your hands of death. With so many thousands of dead salmon, the men who counted and collected their dead bodies literally could not wash themselves clean of death for weeks."

This play also created new, deeper understandings for non-Native community members. After one of the performances a woman told how she had heard the news on the radio about the fish kill but that she just "didn't fully get it . . . how devastating it was for Native communities." She told us that the play helped her understand the emotional and spiritual significance of the event, and that she felt a sense of loss for the first time. Her experience was echoed by many other non-Native audience members. A commercial fisherman told us, "I have long felt this resource [salmon] must be preserved and not exploited to extinction. I would prefer to lose the privilege to fish salmon so that the Native people maintain their lifestyle." A university student likened the fish kill to the Katrina crisis in New Orleans, making connections between a predicted ecological disaster, government failure, and issues of racism. Lastly, a community activist relayed that the portrayal of the rancher working in solidarity with the Native community made him feel hopeful. He had been feeling hopeless about the possibility of ranchers, farmers, the government, and corporations shifting their perspectives.

Overall, the tour was a success but was not without its challenges. As the director and production manager I was often pulled in many directions. Like all touring productions, ours involved unexpected hiccups along the way. We had problems with sound systems, lights, and locks at the different performance spaces. We had limited and oddly configured "stages" that lacked exits. For our Karuk performance, all of our blocks and props, including the salmon, went missing from our storage space. Two actors pulled out of our last show, leaving me and my colleague Jaese Lecuyer to perform their roles, scripts in hand. Quick problem solving and flexibility were necessary each time we entered a new space.

The challenges and mishaps in touring only seemed to bring the group closer together. Once again humor acted as good medicine for these minor "crises." In the end, it was the Native community who really stepped up to help make these productions happen. Marlette Grant-Jackson (Yurok) created our posters, while Judy Risling oversaw our finances. Mary Campbell's entire family helped hang posters and get the word out for the Hupa performance. KIDE, a Hupa community radio station, gave us an interview to promote the play just minutes after we walked into the station. Margaret (Maggie) Lee Peters, a Yurok-Karuk and Ish-Kaysh's mom, sold sweets and put out a donation jar to help fund our tour. She also gave us important feedback during some of our rehearsals, while Jennifer Burgess (Hupa) assisted us in every way possible throughout the rehearsal and performance process. In the end, bringing the show to the reservation allowed for greater participation and integration of the Native community into all aspects of the production. Like the salmon, we completed the cycle by returning to the source. Together we brought the story of the salmon back home.

When I reflect on the years of organizing, sharing, and working together with everyone on the KTP, I recognize how fortunate I was to be a part of this project. I was part of dialogue and collaboration that does not happen often enough; Native people and non-Native people seeking common ground. I began to understand that my community extended well beyond the town of Arcata to include the Yurok, Hupa, and Karuk communities. The individualist worldview in which I was raised had been cracked open. Through this project I began to realize that we, the Native and non-Native communities, ultimately have a shared story, a shared loss, and a shared responsibility.

The *Salmon Is Everything* project has taught me that the telling of our stories can ultimately change our lives and the communities in which we live. Writer, artist, and activist Jeannette Armstrong (Okanagan) speaks to this power of storytelling:

> Speaking is a sacred act in that words contain spirit, a power waiting to become activated and become physical. Words do so upon being spoken and create cause and effect in human interaction. What we speak determines our interactions. Realization of the power of speaking is in the realization that words can change the future and in the realization that we have that power.[46]

The possibility that I may witness several dams from the Klamath River removed in the years to come once again reaffirms my commitment to my community and to theatre as a vehicle for change. I look forward to witnessing the wild salmon swimming freely upstream and to once again seeing the Yurok, Karuk, and Hupa fishnets heavy with catch.

STORY, SOVEREIGNTY, RELATION, AND PLACE

Teaching *Salmon Is Everything* in the Contexts of the Indigenous Environmental Movement

Kirby Brown

SETTING THE STAGE

On October 27, 2016, a Portland, Oregon, jury exonerated seven defendants charged in the forty-one-day armed occupation of the Malheur Wildlife Refuge. After six months of testimony, only six hours of deliberations, and the ninth-hour replacement of a juror, the jury was unable to reach the unanimous verdict required to convict, despite indisputable evidence that the defendants were in fact guilty of every single charge. This was nothing new for the Bundys, however, as the Malheur occupation was only months removed from the Nevada standoff during which dozens of white settler "patriots" led by Cliven Bundy took up arms against Bureau of Land Management and other officials over their refusal to pay miniscule cattle grazing fees on claims of constitutional rights to the "open ranges" of the west. Never mind that no such rights actually exist, that taking up arms against federal officials constitutes insurrection, or that claims to "open range" rights on "public" lands were made possible by the forcible dispossession of the region's First Peoples, the Burns-Paiute tribal nation. As former council person Jarvis Kennedy commented at the time, "It doesn't matter what they say. We were here before the whites, we're here now, and we'll be here when they're gone. This will always be Paiute land."[47] Kennedy's claim to presence not only interrupts settler narratives of "popular sovereignty," but also makes visible the ignorance, erasure, revisionism, and cynicism upon which those claims necessarily rest.

Events taking place halfway across the country at Standing Rock, North Dakota, brought these dynamics into sharp relief. Present in small numbers since May 2016, a growing coalition of Standing Rock tribal citizens, extended relations of *Oceti Sakowin*, and Indigenous and non-Indigenous allies came together to contest one of the most egregious cases of environmental racism in recent memory—the rerouting of the Dakota Access Pipeline (DAPL) from just outside the predominantly white state capital of Bismarck to one mile west of the Standing Rock Sioux reservation. Anchored to legitimate claims to treaty and human rights, water protectors employed ceremonially grounded, nonviolent, direct-action tactics in order to stop the construction of DAPL across unceded Sioux treaty lands, to protect sites of cultural and spiritual significance, and to safeguard rights to clean water throughout the watershed. Unlike the relatively banal response to the armed occupiers at Malheur, *un*armed men, women, children, and elders were confronted with an overwhelming show of violent force by public and private police. In a situation more reminiscent of 1890 than of 2016, one commenter on Twitter accurately noted, "The Sioux are literally being forced at gunpoint to accept ecological risks that North Dakota's white residents refused."[48] If the water protectors' rallying cry, *Mni Wiconi*, reminded us that water is life and that we are all downstream from somewhere, the divergent responses to Malheur and Standing Rock highlighted the extent to which Indigenous lives and lands remain expendable in the face of fossil fuel development and the politics of big oil, agriculture, and industry.

As I attempted to make sense of these issues and so many others like them across Indian Country, I was compelled to work them explicitly into my classrooms the following term. Specifically, I was interested in exploring not just the historical, social, and political contexts out of which these conflicts emerged—an approach I use in all of my courses on Native American literature and film—but also the complicated relationships between story, sovereignty, relationality, and place that inform how stakeholders from all sides understand, represent, and act upon those contexts. I was especially drawn to the explosion of visual art and new media coming out of the NoDAPL movement and decided to organize the course around the question of how literature, music, art, and performance might advance contemporary struggles for Indigenous sovereignty, self-determination, and environmental justice. As an enrolled citizen of the Cherokee Nation of Oklahoma living and working in *Kalapuya Ilihi*—the ancestral homelands and political territories of the Kalapuya people, now part of the Confederated Tribes of Grand Ronde and Siletz—it was also important for me to ground the course in the histories, cultures, places, and contemporary experiences of the Indigenous peoples of the region. After consulting with Indigenous students and colleagues about potential approaches, I focused the second half of the course on issues of resource allocation, dam removal, salmon restoration, and cultural revitalization in the Klamath River Basin. Because I had come to know Theresa May as a conscientious non-Native colleague with strong commitments to Indigenous peoples and to issues of environmental and social justice, I chose *Salmon is Everything: Community-Based Theatre in the Klamath Watershed* to anchor the unit.

ACT I: PLAY-AS-LITERARY TEXT

Considering the erasure of Burns-Paiute presence in coverage of the Malheur occupation and of Sioux treaty and territorial rights grounding demonstrations at Standing Rock, I realized that providing students with adequate contexts in which to locate their own engagements with the play would be crucial. *Salmon Is Everything* usefully provides an abundance of such materials. The foreword by Gordon Bettles, a Klamath tribal member and longtime steward of the Many Nations Longhouse at the University of Oregon, grounds the play in Klamath creation narratives, longstanding cultural practices, and contemporary histories of dispossession, termination, and efforts toward restoration and revitalization. The introduction that follows, written by May, provides a detailed, accessibly written account of the topography and ecology of the watershed; the multiple Indigenous communities who have lived in and managed the region from time immemorial; and the legal and political mechanisms that led to massive dam projects for agricultural use which contributed to the horrific fish kill that animates the play. Accounts by educator Suzanne M. Burcell and environmental management expert Kathleen McCovey, both Karuk women and central collaborators on the play, provide further cultural, historical, and personal contexts about the play's production, its impacts on the tribal communities that saw it, and how both women came to understand the challenges and possibilities of socially committed theatre. Two pieces by May and codirector Jean O'Hara provide important non-Native perspectives on the transformative experience of working on the play and what it means to come into relationship with Indigenous peoples, places, stories, and experiences as settler scholar-artists. Additionally, students also researched and facilitated discussions of many of the numerous other resources listed in the bibliography and mentioned throughout the play—from treaties, legislative actions, and legal decisions to newspaper articles and government reports to video documentaries and tribal cultural-ecological studies.

For students whose only historical frame of reference for the Pacific Northwest is Lewis and Clark, the Oregon Trail, or celebrationist treatments of the pioneer ethos, such reorientations unsettle "commonsense" colonialist claims to history and place; resituate Indigenous peoples and cultural practices within an explicitly contemporary context; and map productive relationships between Native and non-Native peoples united around a common cause informed by Indigenous voices and cultural frameworks. Just as the play is structured around a diversity of voices and experiences, the accompanying materials similarly highlight the collaborative, collective nature of the theatrical project and of environmental justice movements more broadly. Having students research and facilitate discussions around these and other secondary materials embeds them in these dynamics, allowing them to join the collaborative effort while also coming to terms with their own relationships to the histories and experiences the play dramatizes. As a Native educator in a predominantly white institution steeped in Pioneer hagiography and celebrations of discovery and settlement, I can't emphasize enough how important such re-framings are not simply to introduce and contextualize the play, but also to provide students—both Native and non-Native—various points of entry, identification, and accountability to the play and to one another.

These dynamics are embedded in the production and structure of the play itself. As a community-centered project between a non-Indigenous scholar-playwright and the Indigenous communities about which she writes, *Salmon Is Everything* models the kind of intercultural dialog and exchange crucial to contemporary struggles over sovereignty and self-determination. These commitments are evident not only in the collaborative, recursive production of the text itself, illustrated in the commentaries by May, Burcell, McCovey, and O'Hara mentioned above, but also in the development of character relationships and the ways they variously come to terms with one another and with contested understandings of history and place that organize the play. The opening scene literally sets the stage with these dynamics, presenting readers, audiences, and students with a wide array of stakeholders possessing various relationships to the watershed—from Klamath, Modoc, Yurok, Karuk, and Hupa families and communities who have lived there since time immemorial; to settler farmers, ranchers, loggers, and religious figures with generational ties to the region; to university environmental researchers, outdoor recreation workers, seasonal tourists, politicians, and reporters from a host of racial, ethnic, cultural, class, and gender backgrounds. Framed by visual and audio effects capturing the sights and sounds of the landscape and the River, projected images of Salmon, and the presence of a Salmon Dancer throughout, what emerges is a multiply-populated space of human and non-human relations, diverse and different, yes, but always informed by the lifeways and cultural practices of the First Peoples of the region.[49]

The second scene, "Salmon is Family," illustrates these commitments, grounding the play specifically in Karuk and Yurok cultural practices as viewed through one modern-day Karuk-Yurok family. The opening stage directions set a scene for students that refuses romantic narratives of vanishing Indians or understandings of contemporary Indigenous life framed by popular assumptions of damage, deficit, or tragedy:

> Late summer. The sound of laughter; actors in a pool of light go through motions of working—hauling in nets, cleaning fish, canning smoked fish; children play on the floor. The mood is joy, excitement. JULIE and WILL have an eight-month-old baby, who sleeps in a traditional cradleboard; LOUISE has two children, a boy and girl ages for and ten. Dialogue often overlaps; speaking easily and playfully as they invoke memories and tell stories for the benefit of the children. (36)

Rather than broken Nations made of broken families composed of broken individuals alienated from culture and from one another, *Salmon Is Everything* presents audiences and readers with a joyful family making themselves whole again and again through fellowship, laughter, story, and ongoing cultural practice. The opening lines of the scene, spoken by Julie, her grandmother Rose, her auntie Louise, and her husband Will, reorient student-readers/viewers to a different set of values and relationships which organize the play: "When we do this work we are giving thanks to the Creator for the Salmon, for the River. Salmon is the center of our world, our heart, our sustenance . . . Salmon is our family . . . Salmon are the spirits of our ancestors, *c'iyals* come back to give life to everything" (36). As the exchange continues, we watch and listen as this extended family of Karuk-Yurok relatives trade memories, share experiences, and crack jokes, all the while transmitting cultural and familial knowledge—including the use of tribal languages!—across generations.

As Will and Johnny recall how they were each educated into Yurok fishing and boating practices, they also provide readers and viewers with a roadmap of sorts for how to receive the play: "That's how I learned, from watching my uncles, my cousins, people that are older than me. I just watched. People don't have to tell me how to do stuff step-by-step. I just watch . . . If you're a good listener and watch everything, you'll be good at it" (37). The obvious, yet subtle, point delivered here isn't to alert readers or audiences to "insider," ethnographic knowledge of "Indian culture." Rather, it is an invitation to watch and listen attentively and, in doing so, to perhaps come to see the world differently. Rather than viewing Salmon as a commodity, resource, or object of environmental preservation, for instance, this framing scene introduces the multiple other ways this family and tribal communities across the watershed relate to them—as sustenance, culture, history, humility, gratitude, and kin; indeed, as the stuff of life itself. Punctuated by the recent arrival of a new addition to the family, the community, and the nation, this opening vignette signals not simply the survival or continuance of Indigenous lifeways on the Klamath, but their ongoing perpetuation into the future.

It is perhaps because of this early image of health, wholeness, and futurity that the full weight of the fish kill dramatized later in the play is rendered visible for audiences, readers, and students. Appropriately titled "Lamentation," scene 9 recalls the shock, horror, rage, devastation, and grief experienced by the community upon learning of the massive loss of life. Coming on the heels of the Jump Dance ceremony marking the return of the Salmon and the renewal of life, the reality of the fish kill devastated tribal peoples up and down the Klamath. As Kathleen McCovey notes in her contribution to the volume, "This is the part of the production where the people realize what is happening to the Salmon; the people realize that their relatives are lying along the riverbank suffocating and there is nothing the people can do to help the Salmon People" (97). In order to drive this point home, the scene contrasts the intense emotion and intimacy expressed by the tribal community with the journalistic presentation of "facts" related by a non-Native reporter who has arrived on the scene to document the carnage. Punctuating and eventually overwhelming the reporter's "nuts-and-bolts" commentary, Karuk and Yurok characters collectively communicate the impact of the catastrophe as they ceremonially mark the scale of death and loss which met their relatives on their long-awaited return. As the numbers rise from thirty to forty to fifty to sixty to "seventy thousand dead," tribal members recall the intimacies of the violence they were forced to witness and participate in—from cutting off tails in order to get an accurate count of the devastation to slashing open bodies in order to prevent rot and disease—"each its own shipwreck of life . . . each not only a meal but a life" (53). A symbolic Salmon passed between characters throughout the scene and a background ceremonial song of loss and lament amplify the intimacy and intensity of the scene. Rose's comments perhaps best capture the stakes of the loss as she achingly wonders aloud, "As if these sweet ones are litter, not corpses of our underwater families . . . Who picked up these dead and dying ones?" (53). Contrasting the image of health and wholeness evident in scene 2, scene 9 frames the fish kill as an apocalyptic loss not just of a resource but of the very stuff of life itself. As Rose notes in the final words of the scene, the fish kill was a formative experience with intergenerational implications. "We carry them still," she says, "In our arms, on our backs, in our hearts" (54). The remainder of the play explores how tribal peoples came to terms with that loss, and the possibilities for Native and non-Native residents across the watershed—as well as attentive readers and listeners—to come together across difference in order to prevent this and other losses from happening again in the future.

Indeed, if the opening "Procession" marks the enormous diversity and difference between the characters as they arrive onstage, it also reminds us of commonalities that speak across those differences. Whether as mothers, fathers, children, and extended kin; as husbands and wives; as spiritual leaders, culture-bearers, and land-stewards; or as weavers, music enthusiasts, dancers, and artists/artisans of all ages, these shared experiences and commitments provide the foundation for the various acts of intercultural dialog, mutual exchange, and at least the possibility for reconciliation modeled in later scenes.

For instance, following a hostile back-and-forth between stakeholders at a town hall meeting in scene 12, Julie, a Karuk-Yurok woman, and Tim, a third-generation white farmer, run into one another outside of the meeting and open a conversation mediated by a humorous exchange about parenting and children. As small talk transitions into a discussion about solutions to seemingly intractable conflicts, Tim offers to visit Julie and her husband Will, a Yurok-Karuk fisherman, at their home in order to try and come to some understanding of the impact of the fish kill on their family and community. After a heated confrontation in scene 15 during which Will challenges Tim to hold himself and his fellow farmers accountable for their role in the genocidal implications of the kill, Tim arrives at a more complicated understanding of his relationship to the River and to his Indigenous neighbors. In scene 18, "Captain Jack's Stronghold," Tim finds himself at the site in Lava Beds National Monument where fifty-one Modoc warriors and their families held off the full weight of the US Army for an entire winter before finally being starved into surrender. Offering tobacco "respectfully, in manner of the Native people he knows," Tim addresses the audience, noting: "All the Modocs wanted . . . all Captain Jack wanted was for his people 'to live unmolested on their homeland.' They just wanted to be safe, just like me, just like you" (83). In the following two scenes, Tim convinces his mother Alice (a product of her times who expresses more than a little settler self-entitlement and anti-Indianism in the beginning) of the necessity of working with tribal communities to better manage resources and prioritize the health of the salmon, and approaches Julie with an offer to broker talks with other farmers in the valley. As a non-Native man with generational connections to the land, Tim's character and arc of development provides a point of identification for non-Native readers, audiences, and students while also modeling one vision of what cooperation, collaboration, and allyship might look like.

Other instances of intercultural exchange provide further points of identification and potential avenues for cooperation and collaboration. Through her relationships and interactions with Julie and other Indigenous peoples in the area, Kate, a white university student studying ecological impacts on the river, moves from a strictly scientific understanding of dynamics in the watershed to a more relational understanding of the innate intelligence of Salmon and of the River basin informed by Karuk and Yurok lifeways. In scene 8, as the voices of the Salmon and the Land speak all around her and as the Salmon Dancer moves into and out of the scene, Kate observes, "Sometimes it hits me when I'm out here checking the equipment, trying to gather information to protect them: they are knowledge, they embody it . . . for the tribes, Salmon is everything" (50). From this moment forward, Kate becomes an advocate for both environmental sustainability and for the health and security of the Salmon and the tribal communities for whom it is so significant. For readers, viewers, and students possessing similar environmental commitments, Kate's epiphany makes clear the inextricable connections between environmental health and Indigenous cultural, spiritual, political, and territorial sovereignty. In a related example, Kate's partner Rachel, a photographer of Jewish descent, begins to understand the trauma experienced by Yurok, Karuk, and Klamath peoples at the massive loss of life "of these sweet ones . . . these dead and dying ones" (Rose, 53) via her own family's history of genocidal violence and loss during the Holocaust. Though distinct in time and place, these shared experiences of collective loss—a parallel often drawn by many contemporary Native writers—opens a space in scene 11 for empathy and mourning with Julie, her grandmother Rose, and her auntie Louise, as well as for respect, humor, and appreciation for the beauty and resilience of Karuk and Yurok life.

Even the reporter begins to frame his coverage of the event differently. Upon his first appearance in scene 5, the reporter's language reflects the distance and "big picture" commitments to journalistic objectivity that define the profession. Scene 9, "Lamentation," during which the reporter's voice initially competes with but is ultimately overcome and silenced by Indigenous characters attempting to come to terms with the scale and impact of the loss, demonstrates the utter failure of conventional media coverage to capture the trauma and suffering experienced by Indigenous peoples. By scene 12, informed by his relationship with a Karuk cameraman and his extensive interaction with tribal fishermen and others that take place off-stage, his language shifts from simply mapping out conflicts, stakeholders, and events to a genuine appreciation for the miracle of the Salmon ("Salmon are amazing. Born knowing this river and their place in it. Traveling the same way their ancestors have done for centuries."), and an honest concern for the ways the "situation really hits home" for tribal peoples and, perhaps increasingly, for himself (63).

In these and other examples, *Salmon Is Everything* suggests less a resolution to decades of entrenched conflict along the Klamath than possibilities that intercultural, interpersonal exchange open to partner across difference in good faith and with an eye toward cultivating more empathetic, long-standing relationships across the watershed. This is what strikes me most about the play and what I find most useful in terms of teaching it in a literature classroom: it honestly confronts the very real tensions—some unresolved and perhaps irresolvable—that have informed the cultural politics along the Klamath since the arrival of euroamerican settlers in the nineteenth century without conceding the inevitability of such conflicts—what Bettles accurately terms a collision of cultures in the foreword—or foreclosing possibilities for transformative change. As Tim notes in the final scene, "This is just a start. We've got a lot of people up here that'll be tough to convince because they're afraid" (88). Ongoing efforts by a wide consortium of local stakeholders and corporate partners to sidestep state and national politics in order to effect a hard-won program of dam removal, salmon restoration, and collective resource allocation and management suggests all that remains to be done and the very real possibilities of collectively imagining it into being.

ACT II: TEXT-AS-EMBODIED PERFORMANCE

While having students engage these issues through facilitations, discussions, free writes, discussion forums, and literary-formal analyses provided various avenues for students to come to an intellectual understanding of the issues at work in the play-as-text, it was not until they had an opportunity to embody the text-as-performance in the Many Nations Longhouse that it came to life for many of them. This came about as a collaborative effort between my own undergraduate class on art, literature, and Indigenous political movements and Theresa's dual-level, undergraduate-graduate course on contemporary Indigenous theatre. After making the decision to use the text, I reached out to Theresa to see if she might also be willing include the play in her course and to combine our classes for some performance work in the Longhouse. She enthusiastically agreed, and we had the great fortune of having Marta Clifford, Grand Ronde tribal member and the actor who played Rose in the University of Oregon production, along for the ride as well. So our classes met collectively together for two days and worked our way through many of the scenes discussed above. Exposing literature and drama students to the dynamics of embodiment, performance, collaboration, and community-building across courses and disciplines allowed us to embody much of the work the play itself does through dramatic technique and stagecraft. That it took place in the Many Nations Longhouse was crucial to this experiment.

Prior to combining our classes, my class had the good fortune of being hosted by Gordon Bettles in the Longhouse just prior to reading the play. For many students, this was their first visit to the Longhouse, and so part of the work Gordon did for us was to situate us in relation to this new place where we gathered. He began by introducing himself according to Klamath protocols in the Klamath language. He then translated what he had said and explained that he begins this way in order that others might know him not simply as the Longhouse Steward or a UO Alum, but, more importantly, in relation to the people, places, histories, and extended relations of his family and community. He next walked us through the history of the Longhouse and of Native peoples on campus. Beginning with the cultural significance of the Longhouse's layout and construction, Gordon educated us on the protocols, expectations, and responsibilities that govern relationships there. These include principles of hospitality, equality, reciprocity, respect, and always coming into the space with a clean body (no alcohol or drugs), a good heart (leave hostility at the door), and an open mind (welcome influence from others)—values that also structure the play. He then led us in a Klamath song that roughly translates as "I Change You, You Change Me." Doing so, he explained, was not simply to foster good will among people, but also to extend the same kind of care, respect, and gratitude to the Longhouse for the refuge it offers and the opportunities it affords to come together in fellowship and intellectual exchange. In order to drive home these commitments, Gordon gifted us with a few Klamath oral histories on the creation of the world by Gmok'umc, on the emergence of the Klamath people, and on their relationships to Salmon, *c'wam*, and other non-human kin throughout the watershed. Just as the play offers Indigenous alternatives for what it means to come into relation with place, our visit to the Longhouse also afforded students with a culturally-grounded, place-based understanding of what it means to do intellectual work in relation to *Kalapuya Ilihi* and to tribal peoples on campus and across the state. In subsequent conversations, discussion posts, and course evaluations, students routinely highlighted the visit to the Longhouse as one of the more transformative moments of the course.

It also provided an important framework to ground our interactions with the play in the classroom and, later, as embodied practice/performance. As we arrived to Longhouse the next week, I reminded students of the protocols Gordon had shared with us and encouraged them to approach him, shake his hand, and introduce themselves. Both Theresa and I then did the same thing, moving about the room and making sure to welcome students from both classes to the space. Gordon then offered a blessing for the work we were going to do over the next couple of days and led us in a few rounds of "I Change You, You Change Me," teasing us for singing timidly like "Beavers" rather than strong and assertive like the "Ducks" we were (which drew more than a few guffaws across the space). Theresa then led us through a series of dramatic warm-up exercises designed to prime our voices, to loosen up our bodies, to model active listening and honest response, and to overcome any sense of self-consciousness, anxiety, or nervousness about performance. While the drama students threw themselves easily into these exercises, those in my literature class were more cautious. As we moved about the space pairing off with different partners and sharing equally in the silliness and hilarity of our movements and surroundings, many of them gradually began to open themselves up to the possibilities of performance and of making oneself vulnerable to others.

Dramatizations of three scenes in particular captured these dynamics for Native and non-Native students alike. In the first, "Telemetry," we invited a Klamath student from my class to play the role of Yurok-Karuk undergraduate Julie and a non-Native graduate student from Theresa's course to take on the role of Kate, a well-meaning, white liberal graduate student in environmental studies. The scene opens with Kate and Andy, their professor, showing Julie how to place temperature monitors and tracking devices on Salmon in order better to document the ecological shifts taking place in the River. As it continues, tension builds between the two women as Julie believes that her people already know what's wrong with the river (dams, agricultural irrigation) and possess the Indigenous knowledge to remedy the situation. The problem, as she sees it, is that bureaucrats and government agencies don't value that knowledge. Kate sympathizes and informs Julie about an upcoming stakeholders meeting, encouraging her to attend. Unable to contain her frustration, anger, and pain any longer, Julie admonishes Kate not to tell her what to do and instructs her in the very different stakes in play for her family and community:

> [F]or us the threat of extermination is immediate, just like it is for the fish. You come here doing your research that will eventually get you some good agency job. You care, sure, but if the Salmon go extinct, you'll find some other species to save. For my family, if the Salmon don't survive my grandmother will

> die of a broken spirit. You called that fish "Brother" . . . but it's a metaphor for you. It's *not a metaphor* for us! My people have lived here for ten thousand years of more . . . My people live here. They die here! They are the trees, the water, the fish. That the Salmon are brothers is not some kind of myth; the Salmon are not symbolic of life, they are life . . . If the Salmon die, we break apart; the Salmon make life make sense! (46)

After this, Kate leaves the scene but not before reminding Julie that she's speaking to the choir and that others need to hear what she has to say. Though still angry, Julie takes Kate's message to heart and eventually begins to participate in community discussions. For her part, Kate, as discussed above, comes to a very different understanding of the relationships between environmental health, settler colonialism, and tribal sovereignty.

The scene turns on the building tension between the two and how each come to understand their responsibilities in the struggle differently. It requires the actor playing Julie to demonstrate a kind of repressed frustration that is eventually projected entirely onto Kate. In turn, the actor playing Kate has to capture that well-meaning, "expert" condescension which often organizes relationships between academics and Native peoples. We had the students read through the scene one time and asked others in the room to identify the important beats, or moments, in the scene. We then had them "play" the scene through from start to finish and debriefed collectively afterward. While students thought that the actor playing Kate more or less captured the dynamics of her character, we all encouraged the actor playing Julie to give herself over to the frustration, anger, and emotion expressed in the dialog. As a naturally pensive, quiet, and soft-spoken Klamath woman, she admitted to having difficulty accessing that emotional space in public. We briefly stepped aside with one another as Theresa continued to lead the larger discussion, and I asked her if any of Julie's experience resonated with her which, as a young Klamath woman, they did. I invited her to draw upon those experiences in the moments leading into the scene and to open herself to expressing whatever emotions began to rise to the surface, to simply "be present" with them provided she felt safe doing so. She agreed to give it another go and as they arrived at the climactic moment, there was a palpable difference in the room. The student later commented that at some point she no longer felt like an actor reading a part and playing a role; rather, she took Julie's words and spoke them as honestly as she could from her own experience as a young Klamath woman. The effect on the non-Native student playing Kate was powerful, and by the third time through both inhabited the kind of theatrical immediacy the scene demands. As the scene drew to its close, the other students erupted in applause, affirming both the success and the theatrical significance of their efforts.

Another scene, "The Visit," created similar opportunities to explore the dramatic possibilities of playing scenes, particular exchanges, and specific line deliveries in a variety of ways. For example, a Karuk graduate student in theatre played the role of Will, a Yurok-Karuk fisherman more than a little suspicious of overtures by Tim (played by a non-Native theatre student) for dialog and exchange. Like the Klamath student mentioned previously, the Karuk graduate student possessed an intimate knowledge of the issues organizing the play and had no problem mobilizing the anger and rage Will expresses in the scene. In fact, as Will's challenge that Tim and all non-Native farmers accept their role in precipitating what for him is an act of literal and cultural genocide—"This is a real-life situation. It's not a book; it's not pretend. It's not something you read about that happened a hundred years ago. It's happening right now, today. To people in my life" (77)—the actor playing Tim wound up playing him rather passively, almost as if he was cowed by the experience. As we discussed the scene collectively, and as each actor communicated what they were going for, some students suggested that playing Will exclusively via anger missed the anguish, pain, and sadness that also informs his character. In doing so, Tim emerged, unexpectedly, as the "victim," which we all agreed was decidedly not the point of the scene. The next time through, the actor playing Will began the scene similarly, steeped in sarcasm and a biting dismissal of Tim's motivations. As he proceeded into the most important passage, however, anger and hostility subtly gave way to what some later described as "heartbreak" and "helplessness." There was rage there, to be sure, but this time through it was contextualized by a host of other emotions working on Will's character, emotions that registered physically in the actor's visible embodiment of frustration, exhaustion, and pain. After calling "scene," the student-audience agreed that the shift in performance lent both characters the kind of complexity and emotional spectrum capable of capturing the very real differences that exist between them, while also highlighting their mutual commitments to the health and future of the watershed. One student even commented on the parallel between their unresolved tension and the unresolved situation along the Klamath in our contemporary moment. When pressed on a subsequent discussion forum about why the play left Will and Tim at personal loggerheads, the student replied, "Because to somehow magically make them friends would be so cliché. The point isn't to make everyone friends. The point is to dramatize the conflicts onstage and to open up possibilities for collective action despite them." I couldn't have said it better myself.

While these and other exercises afforded opportunities for the larger class to consider the dynamics of performance from their position as codirectors and audience members, the most important moment in our time together occurred as we collectively staged the play's most heart-wrenching scene, "Lamentation," discussed above. As with other scenes, we read through it once and shared what we thought were its most important features. Students noted the emotional effect generated by the rising body count juxtaposed to the repeated refrain "As they came home," while Theresa, Marta, and I noted the contrast between the sterile language of the reporter's account and the intimacy, anguish, and loss expressed by Karuk, Yurok, and Klamath characters. The next time we read through it, Theresa assigned principle speaking roles to a couple of handfuls of students while the rest of us collectively recited the refrain as we moved about the Longhouse making eye contact as we passed by. This had the effect not only of connecting us more intimately to the actions and words of the play, but also to bring us into literal relationship with one another. As the count rises and the lamentation builds, I noted some students having difficulty speaking their lines or enunciating the refrain. They later shared that the embodied practice not simply of reading lines but of doing so with the expressed intention of connecting with other actors in the room heightened the emotional stakes for them.

Our final read-through accomplished this in spades, as Theresa introduced the replica Salmon mentioned in the stage directions to the dynamic and suggested that we pass it throughout the room as the cast had done in all three productions. As we made our way through the scene a third time, and as the Salmon moved from one student to the next, a number of things happened: principle characters had trouble finishing their lines, the refrain took on a much more somber tone, and many—including myself—became visibly overcome by the weight and mass of the Salmon as it arrived in their hands. Weighing approximately fifteen or twenty pounds, it drew attention to the materiality of the loss, making the rising number of dead and dying and the lamentation of the refrain "come to life," as one student put it. Another commented on how the weight of the Salmon provided a material anchor to the metaphorical "weight" of the loss experienced by Indigenous peoples in the play, a reality that she had understood from an intellectual sense but that hadn't fully "hit home" for her until our time in the Longhouse. Commenting on her own experience playing Rose in the University of Oregon production, Marta recalled similar dynamics taking place onstage with cast members becoming lost in, and at times overwhelmed by, the emotion of the performance. One of my non-Native students, in a comment on a course evaluation, perhaps summed it up best, noting, "I have read drama before and I have attended theatrical performances around histories and experiences very different from my own. I have even been moved by them, as I was by this play. But it wasn't until seeing it performed and then becoming a part of that performance with the rest of the class in the Many Nations Longhouse that I feel like I have some sense of the stakes of what's going on along the Klamath. I realize now that this isn't just a Native problem or a farmer's problem; it's all of our problem." Though the student expressed hesitation about what to do moving forward, he nonetheless expressed gratitude that he had been exposed to histories and perspectives on the issue with which he was previously unfamiliar.

EPILOGUE

It is here—in imagining, dramatizing, and performing alternatives to intractable conflict—that *Salmon Is Everything* does its most important work. Rather than frame the play as a battle between romantic ecological Indians and exploitative white settlers, the play presents a wide cross-section of values and beliefs within and across Indigenous and non-Indigenous communities. This approach allows the play to maintain an empathetic attitude toward its principle characters without romanticizing or vilifying any of them. There are no heroes or villains here, just complex characters—like each of us in the Longhouse that week—working doggedly across difference, race (and racism), anger, fear, vulnerability, empathy, and love in order to better understand and relate to one another in what Anishinaabe writer Leanne Simpson terms "this place where we all live and work together."[50]

This is not to say that the play advocates a naïve, colorblind politics of multicultural diversity, however. Far from it. In its emphasis on history, its privileging of Karuk, Yurok, Hupa, and Klamath lifeways and experiences, and its refusal to fully resolve the conflicts that produced the fish kill in the first place, the play calls attention to ongoing efforts to address these and other issues in a more permanent, sustainable way. In this sense, the final scene, "Sacred Is," works less to provide dramatic closure than to remind readers, audiences, and students of the very real stakes of the project for Indigenous peoples and for all life across the watershed. In our contemporary moment of toxic political rhetoric and seemingly intractable conflicts over identity, culture, land use, and resource allocation in Indian Country and across the west, *Salmon Is Everything* offers a performative imaginary for how those conversations might play out differently—onstage, in the classroom, in our daily lives, across the watershed, and throughout our communities. That is a message worth hearing. That is an image worth envisioning. That is a future worth working toward. That, like the Salmon, is everything.

NOTES

FOREWORD

1 In order to reflect cultural understandings, Native contributors have capitalized the terms *River* and *Salmon*.

2 The terms *Hupa* and *Hoopa*: *Hupa* is used when referring to the culture, people, or language. *Hoopa* is used in reference to the Hoopa Valley Tribe, or the town of Hoopa, California.

INTRODUCTION

3 See LeAnne Howe, "Tribalography: The Power of Native Stories," *Journal of Dramatic Theory and Criticism* 14:1 (1999): 117–30.

4 The Klamath River is a federally designated Wild and Scenic River. Its tributaries include the Williamson, Sprague, Sycan, Lost, Scott, Shasta, and Salmon Rivers, as well as the Trinity River, which has had much of its water redirected south for California agriculture.

5 Major dams on the Klamath River (from south to north) are Iron Gate (1962), Fall Creek (1903), Copco 1 and 2 (1917, 1925), J. C. Boyle (1958), Keno (1931), and Link River (1921).

6 The Klamath Tribes website has a detailed account of the history and impact of the 1953 Termination Act. See http://www.klamathtribes.org/background/termination.html.

7 The history summarized briefly here is both extensive and complex, and I urge readers to seek out the many resources that might provide more detailed information and nuanced understanding than this book can encompass. A good place to start is Stephen Most, *River of Renewal: Myth and History in the Klamath Basin* (Seattle: University of Washington Press, 2006).

8 In The *Klamath Knot: Explorations of Myth and Evolution* (Berkeley:

University of California Press, 2003), David Rains Wallace describes the natural history of this region as two strands of geologic fiber tied in a giant knot. While the book tells a compelling geologic story and is useful for its detailed information about flora and fauna, it ignores the Native cultures that have inhabited this region and helped shape its ecosystems. In the epilogue to the second edition, Wallace makes amends, noting that the tribes have "for thousands of years, maintain[ed] forests and fisheries" (149).

9 See Ron Reed and Kari Marie Norgaard, "Salmon Feeds Our People," in *Indigenous Peoples and Conservation: From Rights to Resource Management*, ed. K. Walker Painemilla, A. B. Rylands, A. Woofter, and C. Hughes (Arlington: Conservation International, 2010), 7–16.

10 For many generations, indigenous people have managed the resources on which their culture and traditions depend. For more about how the Karuk, Yurok, and Hupa people manage the land to sustain traditional foods, see the tribal websites listed in the bibliography. See also Mary Christina Wood and Zachary Welcker, "Tribes as Trustees Again (Part I): The Emerging Tribal Role in Conservation Trust Movement." *Harvard Environmental Law Review* 32, no. 1 (2008): 373–432.

11 Yurok people I spoke with often used this image to described the abundance of salmon remembered by elders; it was echoed by my student collaborators after interviewing elders in their communities.

12 Nina Foran Gee's *Springer's Quest: Life of a Pacific Chinook Salmon* (Happy Camp, CA: Naturegraph Publishers, 2009) follows the journey of one imaginary salmon up the Klamath and then the Salmon River, providing a portrait of the interdependence of fish and the larger ecosystems (including human) of the Klamath watershed.

13 See, for example, Jim Lichatowich, *Salmon without Rivers: A History of the Pacific Salmon Crisis* (Washington, DC: Island Press, 1999);

Joseph Cone and Sandy Ridlington, eds., *The Northwest Salmon Crisis: A Documentary History* (Corvallis: Oregon State University Press, 1996); and Dennis Brown, *Salmon Wars: The Battle for the West Coast Salmon Fishery* (Madeira Park, BC: Harbour, 2005).

14 This number reflects official estimates at the time. See Holly Doremus and A. Dan Tarlock, *Water War in the Klamath Basin: Macho Law, Combat Biology, and Dirty Politics* (Washington, DC: Island Press, 2008), as well as the final report of the Yurok Fisheries Program by Michael Belchik, Dave Hillemeier, and Ronnie M. Pierce, "The Klamath River Fish Kill of 2002: Analysis of Contributing Factors" (February 2004), accessed August 7, 2013, http://www.yuroktribe.org/departments/fisheries/documents/FINAL2002FISHKILLREPORTYTFP.pdf. Subsequent published estimates indicate upward of seventy-seven thousand deaths. See Jo Becker and Barton Gellman, "Leaving No Tracks," *Washington Post*, June 27, 2007. The numbers in the play *Salmon Is Everything* reflect the many informal estimates of those living along the Klamath River and are meant to signify not only the actual animals that died, but the looming loss of culture and livelihood.

15 See Iris Marion Young, "Communication and the Other: Beyond Deliberative Democracy." In *Democracy and Difference: Contesting the Boundaries of the Political*, edited by Seyla Benhabib, (Princeton, NJ: Princeton University Press, 1996): 120–36.

16 We have taken our cue from the Living Newspapers of the Federal Theatre Project. Plays such as *Power and Triple-A Plowed Under* are annotated with their information sources. See Arthur Arent and the staff of the *Living Newspaper, Triple-A Plowed Under, Federal Theatre Plays*, vol. 2, edited by Pierre DeRohan (New York: Random House, 1938).

17 See Barry Wayne McCovey Jr., "Fish Kill: For the Yurok, Salmon Is Everything," *News from Native California* 16:2 (Winter 2002): 1–3. The piece was also published in *Indian Country Today*, October 9, 2002.

18 In order to acknowledge and remember the students from Humboldt State's Indian Tribal and Educational Personnel who worked on this project, a portion of royalties from the sale of this book will go to ITEPP to be used as assistance for Native students.

19 Michael Yellow Bird, "What We Want to Be Called: Indigenous Peoples' Perspectives on Racial and Ethnic Identity Labels." *American Indian Quarterly*, 23:2 (Spring, 1999): 1-21.

20 For more about the complex history that lead to the new Klamath River Renewal Corporation, see, Konrad Fisher, "Revised Klamath Agreement signed! New Agreement Bypasses Congress for Dam Removal by 2020," *EcoNews* 46:3 (June/July 2016): 4-8. http://www.yournec.org/sites/default/files/pdf/EcoNews/EcoNews%20JunJul2016-ALL-opt.pdf/ Accessed online January 13, 2018; Craig Tucker, "Klamath Update: Dam Removal Under a New Administration," in *Osprey* Vol. 87 (2017): 13-14. Also see Tucker, "FAQ on Klamath Dam Removal," Karuk Tribe Natural Resources Department, March 22, 2017: http://www.karuk.us/17-03-22KlamathDamFAQ.pdf.

A CALL TO ACTION

21 Official counts estimated thirty-three thousand; however, informal estimates were much higher. The mounting numbers during those weeks in September were synonymous with community grief. That grief, represented in the incantation of numbers, was later expressed in scene 9 of the play. See California Department of Fish and Game, *September 2002 Klamath River Fish-Kill: Final Analysis of Contributing Factors and Impacts* (July 2004), accessed September 26, 2013, http://www.pcffa.org/KlamFishKillFactorsDFGReport.pdf.

I AM KARUK

22 Kishwoof, or *Ligusticum*, is a form of licorice root that grows in the coastal mountains. The root is dug, dried, used as a healing herb, and burned at ceremonies and other occasions.

BECOMING ROSE

23 Contemporary Native and First Nations theatre comprises a burgeoning body of dramatic literature, criticism, and performance theory by indigenous authors and artists. Readers unfamiliar with the field might begin with Diane Glancy, "Further (Farther): Creating Dialogue to Talk about Native American Plays," *Journal of Dramatic Theory and Criticism* 14:1 (Fall 1999): 127-30; *American Indian Theater in Performance: A Reader,* edited by Hanay Geiogamah and Jaye T. Darby (UCLA American Indian Studies Center). 2000; *Seventh Generation: An Anthology of Native American Plays*, edited by Mimi Gisolfi D'Aponte, (New York: Theatre Communications Group, 1999); *Footpaths & Bridges: Voices from the Native American Women Playwrights Archive*, edited by Shirley A. Huston-Findley & Rebecca Howard (Univ. of Michigan Press), 2011; *Staging Coyote's Dream: An Anthology of First Nations Drama in English*, ed. Monique Mojica and Ric Knowles (Toronto: Playwrights Canada Press, 2003); Christy Stanlake, *Native American drama: a Critical Perspective,* (Cambridge, UK: Cambridge University Press, 2009). Also see the websites listed in the bibliography for UCLA's Project Hoop, and Native Voices at the Autry.

THE EDUCATION OF AN ARTIST

24 The importance of first foods has been documented with legal implications. See, for example, Ron Reed and Kari Norgaard, "Salmon Feeds Our People," in *Indigenous Peoples and Conservation: From Rights to Resource Management,* ed. K. Walker Painemilla, A. B. Rylands, A. Woofter, and C. Hughes, (Arlington: Conservation International, 2010): 7–16, which presents groundbreaking research on the dietary rights of tribal people on the Klamath River. Their research argues that the dams themselves have not only hurt fish runs but also constitute a violation of the basic civil rights of Native people.

25 "In two worlds" is a phrase Gordon Bettles, steward of the Many

Nations Longhouse at the University of Oregon, described the way Native students navigate contemporary institutions while maintaining traditional cultural practices..

26 For a book that is informative and accessible, specifically regarding Yurok traditions, see Susan Calla, Sandra Jerabek, and Loren Bommelyn, *Passing the Moon through Thirteen Baskets: A Guide to the Natural Year and Native American Celebrations on the Wild Redwood Coast* (Happy Camp, CA: Naturegraph Publishers, 2005).

27 Community-based theatre defines itself as theatre by, for, and about the community. The process, however, is more complex, as case studies reveal. See, for example, Sonja Kuftinec, *Staging America: Cornerstone and Community-Based Theater* (Carbondale: Southern Illinois University Press, 2003); Susan Haedicke and Tobin Nellhaus, eds., *Performing Democracy: International Perspectives on Urban Community-Based Performance* (Ann Arbor: University of Michigan Press, 2005); and Jan Cohen-Cruz, *Local Acts: Community-Based Performance in the United States* (New Brunswick, NJ: Rutgers University Press, 2005).

28 In the making of Moisés Kaufman's Laramie Project, a company of actors from New York went to Laramie, Wyoming, to conduct interviews and developed a play about the beating death of Matthew Shepard. While the project brought the issue of homophobic hate crimes into the national spotlight, many had concerns about a New York–based director flying to the site of community loss and striking professional pay dirt. Another example closer to my own situation: during the development of *Salmon Is Everything*, news of a project by New York director Ping Chong precipitated a heated thread on a Native theatre e-mail list. At the time, Chong was involved in a project called Native Voices—Secret History, based on interviews with Native citizens of Lawrence, Kansas. On April 30, 2005, one online participant, Dianne Yeahquo Reyner, asked, "What happens after the production ends?" and "Who gets to be author? Will Chong take ownership of this piece because he co-wrote it by choosing and arranging the words of others?"

29 The reference is from an informal conference conversation. For more about Roadside Theatre, or to learn more about community-based theatre and what might be called "best practices," see Linda Frye Burnham, ed., *Performing Communities: Grassroots Ensemble Theaters Deeply Rooted in Eight U.S. Communities* (Oakland, CA: New Village Press, 2006).

30 See the note on page 59 in scene 11 of the play.

31 The mouth of the Klamath was a vibrant and vital fishing site for Yurok people long before first contact. When Euro-American settlers discovered the river's bounty in the 1850s, many sought to establish fisheries and canneries. As Stephen Most tells in *River of Renewal: Myth and History in the Klamath Basin* (Seattle: University of Washington Press, 2006), the 1862 Homestead Act allowed Robert Deniston Hume to build the river's first cannery, employing both white settlers and Native American workers to harvest and process the abundant spring and fall salmon runs. The bridge was constructed in the 1920s and tourism flourished for a while as white sport fishermen came to the Klamath to catch chinooks of up to fifty pounds, as well as steelhead, and other species of salmon. By the 1930s, sportfishing enthusiasts and wilderness preservationists lobbied to close canneries and commercial fishing. In 1933, the state of California closed all fisheries on the Klamath because of a desire to preserve the area's scenic beauty, but also because the salmon runs had dramatically declined.

32 See the note on page 60 in scene 11 of the play.

33 See Cohen-Cruz, *Local Acts*.

34 See LeAnne Howe, "Tribalography: The Power of Native Stories," *Journal of Dramatic Theory and Criticism* 14:1 (Fall 1999): 117–30.

35 For more about the work of Consensus Associates, see http://consensusinstitutes.com/.

36 The Klamath Project refers to a 1906 program initiated by the Bureau of Reclamation under which homesteaders were given land in the Klamath Basin for agricultural development. New

allotments after WWI and WWII added project acreage, while federal funding provided for additional dams to be constructed on the Klamath River. For a detailed history of the project, see the introductory chapters of Doremus and Tarlock, *Water War in the Klamath Basin*.

37 Lauren's comments here come from e-mails she sent after returning from the stakeholder meeting. I also discuss Lauren's story in "Toward Communicative Democracy: Developing Salmon Is Everything," in *The Community Performance Reader*, edited by Petra Kuppers and Gwen Robertson (London: Routledge 2007).

38 See Wood and Welcker, "The Tribes as Trustees," who provide an excellent history and legal framing of both traditional Native land management and its emerging intersection with the contemporary land trust movement.

39 Many farmers and ranchers have worked closely with government agencies to help preserve these vast marshlands. The story is beautifully illustrated in Tupper Ansel Blake, Madeline Graham Blake, and William Kittredge, *Balancing Water: Restoring the Klamath* (Berkeley: University of California Press, 2000). Also see *Yamsi*, Dayton O. Hyde's journal of one year on the Hyde family ranch in the upper Klamath region (New York: Dial Press, 1971).

40 See, for example, Lawrence Fine, Eitan Fishbane, and Or N. Rose, eds., *Jewish Mysticism and the Spiritual Life Classical Texts, Contemporary Reflections* (Woodstock, VT: Jewish Lights Publishing, 2011), or Zalman Schachter-Shalomi and Ronald S. Miller, *From Age-ing to Sage-ing: A Profound New Vision of Growing Older* (New York: Warner Books, 1995).

41 My use of the word "weaving" draws on the work of Lisa Mayo, Gloria Miguel, and Muriel Miguel of Spiderwoman Theatre, who use idea of "storyweaving" and "storying" to describe the process of multivocal authorship, as well as the complex ways in which the tapestry of a play draws connections between people, communities, and the land across time and space. See, for example, Howe, "Tribalography," or Christy Stanlake, *Native American Drama:*

A Critical Perspective (New York: Cambridge University Press, 2009), chapter 6.

42 The Yurok and Hoopa Valley tribes renewed the practice of the annual run in which human runners followed the path of salmon migration upriver. In 2015, the Kalamth tribes joined in, linking 260 miles of spawning grounds. See, http://klamathtribes.org/news/runners-followed-historic-salmon-migration-path-260-miles/.

43 See Jill Dolan, "Performance, Utopia, and the 'Utopian Performative,'" *Theatre Journal* 53:3 (October 2001): 455–79.

THE JOURNEY HOME

44 See Diana Taylor, *The Archive and the Repertoire: Performing Cultural Memory in the Americas* (Durham, NC: Duke University Press, 2003).

45 See Hanay Geiogamah and Jaye T. Darby, eds., *American Indian Theatre in Performance: A Reader.*

46 Quoted in Christy Stanlake, *Native American Drama,* 153.

STORY, SOVEREIGNTY, RELATION, AND PLACE

47 This quote is taken from a public talk Jarvis Kennedy delivered at the Many Nations Longhouse at the University of Oregon on November 3, 2016 entitled "Malheur Occupation: A Native American Perspective."

48 @suntzufuntzu. Twitter post. October 29, 2016, 11:36am. https://twitter.com/suntzufuntzu/status/792449947769511936.

49 As with the play, I have adapted the convention of capitalizing *Salmon*, *River*, and other relevant words in order to reflect their cultural significance and personhood as understood within Yurok, Hupa, Karuk, Klamath, and Modoc lifeways.

50 Leanne Betasamosake Simpson, "The Place Where We All Live and Work Together," from *Native Studies Keywords* edited by Stephanie Nohelani Teves, Andrea Smith, and Michelle Raheja. (Tucson: University of Arizona Press, 2015).

BIBLIOGRAPHY

Adams, Ann. "Investing in a Sustainable Future: Yainix Ranch." *Holistic Management in Practice*, July/August 2005, 5–6.

Allen, Paula Gunn. "The Ceremonial Motion of Indian Time: Long Ago, So Far." In *American Indian Theatre in Performance: A Reader*, edited by Hanay Geiogamah and Jaye Darby, 69–75. Los Angeles: UCLA American Indian Studies Center, 2000.

Arent, Arthur, and the staff of the Living Newspaper. *Triple-A Plowed Under, Federal Theatre Plays*, vol. 2, edited by Pierre DeRohan. New York: Random House, 1938.

Barboza, Tony. "Water War between Klamath River Farmers, Tribes Poised to Erupt." *Los Angeles Times*, May 7, 2013. Accessed May 13, 2013. http://articles.latimes.com/2013/may/07/local/la-me-klamath-20130507.

Becker, Jo, and Barton Gellman. "Leaving No Tracks." *Washington Post*, June 27, 2007. Accessed November 5, 2013. http://blog.washingtonpost.com/cheney/chapters/leaving_no_tracks/.

Belchik, Michael, Dave Hillemeier, and Ronnie M. Pierce. "The Klamath River Fish Kill of 2002: Analysis of Contributing Factors." Yurok Tribal Fisheries Program Final Report, February 2004. Accessed August 7, 2013. http://www.yuroktribe.org/departments/fisheries/documents/FINAL2002FISHKILLREPORTYTFP.pdf.

Bell, Maureen. *Karuk: The Upriver People*. Happy Camp, CA: Naturegraph Publishers, 1991.

Blake, Tupper Ansel, Madeline Graham Blake, and William

Kittredge. *Balancing Water: Restoring the Klamath*. Berkeley: University of California Press, 2000.

Brown, Dennis. *Salmon Wars: The Battle for the West Coast Salmon Fishery*. Madeira Park, BC: Harbour, 2005.

Burnham, Linda Frye, ed. *Performing Communities: Grassroots Ensemble Theaters Deeply Rooted in Eight U.S. Communities.* Oakland, CA: New Village Press, 2006.

Busch, Robert. *Salmon Country: A History of the Pacific Salmon.* Toronto: Key Porter Books, 2000.

California Department of Fish and Game. *September 2002 Klamath River Fish-Kill: Final Analysis of Contributing Factors and Impacts.* July 2004. Accessed September 26, 2013. http://www.pcffa.org/KlamFishKillFactorsDFGReport.pdf.

Calla, Susan, Sandra Jerabek, and Loren Bommelyn. *Passing the Moon through Thirteen Baskets: A Guide to the Natural Year and Native American Celebrations on the Wild Redwood Coast.* Happy Camp, CA: Naturegraph Publishers, 2005.

"Chat Transcript with Ping Chong, Author-Director of *Native Voices—Secret History.*" *Lawrence Journal World*, April 28, 2005.

Cohen-Cruz, Jan. *Local Acts: Community-Based Performance in the United States.* New Brunswick, NJ: Rutgers University Press, 2005.

Cone, Joseph, and Sandy Ridlington, eds. *The Northwest Salmon Crisis: A Documentary History.* Corvallis: Oregon State University Press, 1996.

Conquergood, Dwight. "Performing as a Moral Act: Ethical Dimensions of the Ethnography of Performance." In *Turning Points in Qualitative Research: Tying Knots in a Handkerchief*, edited by Yvonna S. Lincoln and Norman K. Denzin, 351–74. Lanham, MD: Rowman and Littlefield, 2003.

Dolan, Jill. "Performance, Utopia, and the 'Utopian Performative.'" *Theatre Journal* 53, no. 3 (October 2001): 455–79.

Doremus, Holly, and A. Dan Tarlock. *Water War in the Klamath Basin: Macho Law, Combat Biology, and Dirty Politics*. Washington, DC: Island Press, 2008.

Driscoll, John. "Poor Prognosis for Salmon Season." *Times-Standard*, March 10, 2006, A1.

Easthouse, Keith. "The Klamath Whistleblower: An In-Depth Interview." *North Coast Journal*, November 3, 2003. Accessed August 7, 2013. http://www.northcoastjournal.com/111303/cover1113.html.

Fine, Lawrence, Eitan Fishbane, and Or N. Rose, eds. *Jewish Mysticism and the Spiritual Life: Classical Texts, Contemporary Reflections*. Woodstock, VT: Jewish Lights Publishing, 2011.

Fisher, Konrad. "Revised Klamath Agreement signed! New Agreement Bypasses Congress for Dam Removal by 2020." *EcoNews*, Vol 46. No. 3 (June/July 2016): 4-8.Gee, Nina Foran. *Springer's Quest: Life of a Pacific Chinook Salmon*. Happy Camp, CA: Naturegraph Publishers, 2009.

Glancy, Diane, "Further (Farther): Creating Dialogue to Talk about Native American Plays," *Journal of Dramatic Theory and Criticism*, 14:1 (Fall 1999): 127-30; Geiogamah, Hanay, and Jaye T. Darby, eds. *American Indian Theatre in Performance: A Reader*. Los Angeles: UCLA American Indian Studies Center, 2000.

Gisolfi D'Aponte, Mimi, ed. *Seventh Generation: An Anthology of Native American Plays*. New York: Theatre Communications Group, 1999.

Haedicke, Susan, and Tobin Nellhaus, eds. *Performing Democracy: International Perspectives on Urban Community-Based Performance*. Ann Arbor: University of Michigan Press, 2005.

Henderson, Bonnie. "Watershed Moment." *Oregon Quarterly*, Autumn 2012, 26–33.

Howe, LeAnne. "Tribalography: The Power of Native Stories." *Journal of Dramatic Theory and Criticism* 14, no. 1 (1999): 117–30.

Huston-Findley, Shirley A. & Rebecca Howard, eds. *Footpaths & Bridges: Voices from the Native American Women Playwrights Archive*. University of Michigan Press, 2011.

Hyde, Becky Hatfield. "Welcome to the New Millennium in the Klamath Basin: Water, Whiskey, Murder, and Hope." *Terrain.org: A Journal of the Built and Natural Environments*, no. 10 (Fall/Winter 2001). Accessed September 13, 2013. http://www.terrain.org/columns/10/guest.htm.

Hyde, Becky Hatfield. "Yainix Journal." Unpublished manuscript, 2004.

Hyde, Dayton O. *Yamsi: A Heartwarming Journal of One Year on a Wilderness Ranch*. New York: Dial Press, 1971.

Kuftinec, Sonja. *Staging America: Cornerstone and Community-Based Theater*. Carbondale: Southern Illinois University Press, 2003.

Jenkins, Matt. "Peace on the Klamath." *High Country News*, June 23, 2008. Accessed May 13, 2013. http://www.hcn.org/issues/373/17763.

Lichatowich, Jim. *Salmon without Rivers: A History of the Pacific Salmon Crisis*. Washington, DC: Island Press, 1999.

May, Theresa J. "Toward Communicative Democracy: Developing *Salmon Is Everything*." In *The Community Performance Reader*, edited by Petra Kuppers and Gwen Robertson, 153–54. London: Routledge, 2007.

McCovey, Barry Wayne Jr. "Fish Kill: For the Yurok, Salmon Is

Everything." *News from Native California* 16, no. 2 (Winter 2002): 1–3.

Mojica, Monique and Ric Knowles, eds. *Staging Coyote's Dream: An Anthology of First Nations Drama in English.* Toronto: Playwrights Canada Press, 2003.

Montgomery, David R. *King of Fish: The Thousand-Year Run of Salmon.* Cambridge, MA: Perseus Books, 2003.

Most, Stephen. *River of Renewal: Myth and History in the Klamath Basin.* Seattle: University of Washington Press, 2006.

Reed, Ron, and Kari Marie Norgaard. "Salmon Feeds Our People." In *Indigenous Peoples and Conservation: From Rights to Resource Management*, edited by K. Walker Painemilla, A. B. Rylands, A. Woofter, and C. Hughes, 7–16. Arlington: Conservation International, 2010.

Reinelt, Janelle. "Notes for a Radical Democratic Theatre: Productive Crisis and the Challenge of Indeterminacy." In *Staging Resistance: Essays on Political Theatre*, edited by Jeanne Colleran and Jenny S. Spencer, 283–300. Ann Arbor: University of Michigan Press, 1998.

Rymer, Russ. "Reuniting a River." *National Geographic Magazine*, December 2008. Accessed August 7, 2013. http://ngm.nationalgeographic.com/print/2008/12/klamath-river/rymer-text.

"Salmon Experts Pressured to Change Findings." Union of Concerned Scientists. Accessed July 25, 2013. http://www.ucsusa.org/scientific_integrity/abuses_of_science/klamath-river-salmon.html.

Salter, John F. "White Paper on Behalf of the Karuk Tribe of California: A Context Statement Concerning the Effect of the Klamath Hydroelectric Project on Traditional Resource Uses and Cultural Patterns of the Karuk People within the Klamath River

Corridor, 2003." Accessed August 7, 2013. http://www.mkwc.org/publications/fisheries/Karuk%20White%20Paper.pdf.

Schachter-Shalomi, Zalman, and Ronald S. Miller. *From Age-ing to Sage-ing: A Profound New Vision of Growing Older*. New York: Warner Books, 1995.

Simpson, Leanne Betasamosake. "The Place Where We All Live and Work Together," from *Native Studies Keywords*, edited by Stephanie Nohelani Teves, Andrea Smith, and Michelle Raheja. Tucson: University of Arizona Press, 2015

Stanlake, Christy. *Native American Drama: A Critical Perspective*. New York: Cambridge University Press, 2009.

Sullivan, Colin. "Landmark Agreement to Remove 4 Klamath River Dams." *New York Times*, September 30, 2009. Accessed August 13, 2013. http://www.nytimes.com/gwire/2009/09/30/30greenwire-landmark-agreement-to-remove-4-klamath-river-d-72992.html.

Taylor, Diana. *The Archive and the Repertoire: Performing Cultural Memory in the Americas*. Durham, NC: Duke University Press, 2003.

Tucker, Craig. "Klamath Update: Dam Removal Under a New Administration." *Osprey* Vol. 87 (2017): 13-14.

________. Tucker, "FAQ on Klamath Dam Removal," Karuk Tribe Natural Resources Department, March 22, 2017. http://www.karuk.us/17-03-22KlamathDamFAQ.pdf.

Wallace, David Rains. *The Klamath Knot: Explorations of Myth and Evolution*. Berkeley: University of California Press, 2003.

Wolf, Edward C., and Seth Suckerman, eds. *Salmon Nation: People, Fish, and Our Common Home*. Portland, OR: Ecotrust, 2003.

Wood, Mary Christina, and Zachary Welcker. "Tribes as Trustees Again (Part I): The Emerging Tribal Role in Conservation Trust

Movement." *Harvard Environmental Law Review* 32:1 (2008): 373–432.

Yellow Bird, Michael. "What We Want to Be Called: Indigenous Peoples' Perspectives on Racial and Ethnic IdentityLabels." *American Indian Quarterly*, 23:2 (Spring, 1999): 1-21

Young, Iris Marion. "Communication and the Other: Beyond Deliberative Democracy." In *Democracy and Difference: Contesting the Boundaries of the Political*, edited by Seyla Benhabib. Princeton, NJ: Princeton University Press, 1996: 120–36.

ABOUT THE CONTRIBUTORS

GORDON BETTLES is a member of the Klamath Tribes and grew up in Chiloquin. He is director of Native American activities and steward of the Many Nations Longhouse at the University of Oregon, where he teaches and mentors Native American students. He served as cultural adviser for the 2011 production of *Salmon Is Everything*. He has an MA in anthropology from the University of Oregon.

KIRBY BROWN is an Assistant Professor of Native American and Ethnic American Literatures in the Department of English at the University of Oregon and an enrolled citizen of the Cherokee Nation. His research interests include Native American literary, intellectual, and cultural production from the late eighteenth century to the present, Indigenous critical theory, sovereignty/self-determination studies, nationhood/nationalism studies, and genre studies. Essays in contemporary Indigenous critical theory, constitutional criticism in Native literatures, Native interventions in the Western and Modernist Studies have appeared in *Studies in American Indian Literatures*, *Routledge Companion to Native American Literatures*, *Texas Studies in Language and Literatures*, and *Western American Literature*. His current book project, *Stoking the Fire: Nationhood in Early Twentieth Century Cherokee Writing*, forthcoming from University of Oklahoma Press, examines how four Cherokee writers variously remembered, imagined, and enacted Cherokee nationhood in the period between Oklahoma statehood in 1907 and tribal reorganization in the early 1970s.

SUZANNE MARIE BURCELL served as cultural adviser for the Klamath Theatre Project and the 2006 production of *Salmon Is*

Everything. She is an enrolled member of the Karuk Tribe, with a BA in psychology (1978), an MA in business administration (1981), and an MA in education (2004), all from Humboldt State University. She has served Native students and communities as faculty and staff within nonprofit and tribal organizations and post-secondary institutions for thirty-three years. Her contributions to the social and economic development of tribal communities have been recognized by the US Small Business Administration, USDA Forest Service, Economic Development Administration, Karuk Tribe, and Hoopa Valley Tribe. She received Humboldt State's Distinguished Alumni Award in 2000. She lives in Willow Creek, California, and now relishes her current role as full-time grandma.

MARTA LU CLIFFORD is a tribal elder and member of The Confederated Tribes of Grand Ronde (Chinook, Cow Creek, Cree). She currently serves as the Tribal Elder-In-Residence for the University of Oregon Native theatre courses, under the direction of Theresa May. She also assists in coordinating the public readings of Native plays at the Many Nations Longhouse on campus. In 2011 she played Rose in the production of *Salmon Is Everything* at the University of Oregon. She is committed to ensuring Native plays and playwrights are shown, developed, and shared in the community. When she's not busy with Native theatre she works full-time as a procurement counselor with the Oregon Procurement Technical Assistance Center in Springfield, Oregon. She holds an associate's degree from Pioneer Pacific College.

THERESA MAY is an associate professor at the University of Oregon. Her research interests include applied theatre and environmental justice, community-engaged theatre praxis, contemporary Native theatre, twentieth-century American drama, embodiment theory, critical animal studies, and ecodramaturgy. She is cofounder of Earth Matters on Stage (EMOS), an international ecodrama playwright's festival, and coeditor of *Readings in Performance and Ecology*. Her articles have appeared in *Theatre Topics*, *Canadian Theatre Review*, *Journal of Dramatic Theory and Criticism*, and *Journal of American Theatre*. She is coauthor of *Greening Up Our Houses*, on sustainable theatre management. Her current book project, *Ecodramaturgy and the Greening of American Theatre*, tracks the emergence of an environmental sensibility in contemporary American theatre and examines how the representation of environmental ideas on the twentieth century American stage are bound up with ideologies of race, class, and gender. Prior to earning a PhD in theatre history and criticism from the University of Washington, she was artistic director of Theatre in the Wild in Seattle and earned an MFA in acting from the University of Southern California.

KATHLEEN MCCOVEY lives in Happy Camp, California, where she was born and raised in Karuk traditions. Her grandparents, Ernest and Esther Spinks, taught her how to fish, hunt, cure, and prepare meat to be stored for the winter. A Karuk herbalist, Kathy teaches the gathering of edible, medicinal, and ceremonial plants. She has worked as an anthropologist for the US Forest Service since 1990. She earned her BS in archaeology/anthropology from Fresno State University and an MA in environment and community at Humboldt State University. She served as cultural adviser for *Salmon Is Everything* and played the role of Rose in the 2006 and 2007 productions.

JEAN O'HARA recently earned her PhD in theatre and performance studies at York University and teaches at Marlboro College in Vermont. She served as codirector of the 2006 production of *Salmon Is Everything* and as director of the play's 2007 tour up the Klamath River. She has also been a collaborator with Native Earth Performing Arts, the Centre for Indigenous Theatre, the Alianait Arts Festival, the San Francisco Mime Troupe, and the Dell'Arte International School of Physical Theatre. Jean has been directing and teaching theatre for the past fifteen years, with expertise in Augusto Boal's theatre for social justice. Her research interests include Indigenous theatre and representation, and queer performance. She is the editor of *Two-Spirit Acts: Queer Indigenous Performances*, Playwrights Canada Press, 2013.

INDEX

Note: Page references for diagrams are italicized. Note material is indicated by an "n" and followed by back of the book note number.

G

H

I

M